INDEPENDENT FORCE PROTECTION

INDEPENDENT FORCE PROTECTION

PRIVATE SECURITY FOR PREPPERS

Independent Force Protection: Private Security for Preppers

Create Space Independent Publishing Platform

ISBN: 1518876374
ISBN-13: 978-1518876370

ACKNOWLEDGMENTS

To God the Father, the Son, and the Holy Spirit, without Whom I would find no talent, no opportunity, and no friends with which to affect either my trade or my interests.

Deo gratias.

DEDICATION

To all who devote his or her life to defeating evil, wherever it may be found, and protecting innocent human lives wherever they may live.

IN MEMORY OF

To all who have lost their lives because society denied them an opportunity to defend themselves.

TABLE OF CONTENTS

INTRODUCTION

TO PREPARE FOR anything represents an extraordinary effort. To begin with, one must know what it is, precisely, that he or she is preparing for. Secondly, they must understand *how* best to prepare for that potentiality with the focus upon reaching a particular objective satisfactorily. Thirdly, one must be able to recognize the successful completion of that goal lest he or she devote too much time and resources to the effort. Finally, one must not be too relaxed upon achieving that particular purpose just in case subsequent objectives appear.

In this, we can presume that *all* objectives are transitory and that our efforts to affect them merely part of our daily life. That is, humans are a species of planners and goal seekers, despite most of us appearing as if we could not plan our way out of a wet paper bag and our most illustrious goal simply one of avoiding that struggle to begin with. This said, you are reading this book because your primary function remains to live as long as you are reasonably capable of surviving.

Because of this, you have undoubtedly come under a great number of terms, some more conciliatory than others, a few downright slanderous. Prepper, survivalist, fanatic* – all these represent derogatory terms from those bent on life through conveniences and taxpayer-funded services. You, however, do not care much about *what* people call you – they will not be around very long after a major catastrophe anyway. Your revenge rests

---

* For convenience, this book will occasionally employ the terms 'Prepper' or 'Survivalist' for their colloquial recognition, despite the desire to use the more appropriate term of *individual*.

upon knowing that preparation – as with *anything* in life – is simple common sense.

Yours is a life of double-checking door locks, keeping the car's gas tank above half-filled and leaving early for work during inclement weather. You are also a voracious reader, trusting no one to determine your level of knowledge, the best "unlicensed" physician on the planet, and, most of all, the proudest defender of your family. After all, to survive matters little if you cannot take your loved ones along for the journey.

In this regard, you have built your home to remain off the grid (insofar as practical), store months' worth of food, water, and medicine, and keep that archaic Jeep or Land Cruiser well maintained *just in case*. Nevertheless, you may have overlooked the principles of *protecting* your plan to survive, primarily that of keeping your family and your assets secured from aggression and sabotage. That is, despite your being "loaded for bear" and, quite possibly, having had experienced a few actual bear hunts within your life, you may not be adequately prepared to deal with the worst that humanity has to offer.

It remains likely that your concept of security has drawn heavily upon the great multitude of "survivalist", "Prepper", or "doomsday" books that flood the market (and we are not even going to mention Prepper eBooks and Kindle publications for rather obvious reasons), each offering various methods and suggestions for defending your abode or bug out location (BOL). Sadly, these publications remain either too simplistic or too fantastical, ranging from the merely comical to the functionally absurd. Their authors assume that either 1.) You remain too stupid to know the difference between "catastrophe" and "Armageddon" or 2.) That you could never appreciate the difference between defense and protection, security and resting secured.

For the sake of discussion, we can provide the following review of problems associated with these books:

♦ *They consider the concept of preparation to involve "end of world" scenarios, often built upon the foundation of apocalyptic tradition.* Let's face it, 'civilization' has *been* around for about 10,000 years, give or take a century and it will continue for long after you and your friends have settled back into dust. True, Grecian, Roman, Egyptian, Aztec, Mayan, etc. civilizations have disappeared, but they did not preclude the United States and others from arising either. Therefore, while we may not expect the United States, Russia, China, or Andorra to be around 500 years from now, we should not rule out that *humans* would not be.

♦ *They consider Government as the enemy of preppers and survivalists.* Even the most powerful nation in history, the United States of America, cannot keep trains running on time. Or provide care for its military veterans. With the increase in the global population and the reduction of tax revenues, governments around the world have become bloated, inefficient, and bureaucratic. We can, therefore, largely ignore the thoughts of "black helicopters" or "men in black" knocking upon our front door to take away our rights. Their constituencies on several orders of magnitude outnumbered even the most tyrannical governments in history. What makes the 21st century different, however, rests with globalization and an inability to keep *anything* secret for long.

♦ *They spend too much time dealing with such ridiculousness as "zombies" or mutant creatures.* The only zombies that you will encounter rest at the bar during Happy Hour. Enough said.

♦ *Their concept of security and defense rests upon 'fire fights' with equally power adversaries.* You will *not* last long – seasoned prepper or not – if you plan to conduct combat operations during the course of the future. *Someone* will destroy you – eventually.

♦ *Current books single out a particular crisis or suggest that you need to plan for every conceivable eventuality.* Survival is *not* an academic program where the reader can specialize within a particular field conducive to his or her interests. Nor does it mean that, since you can weather (no pun intended) a hurricane, you may further survive an earthquake or volcano. As with everything within life, success means that you understand your weaknesses and strengths and proceed according to the best utilization of these attributes.

For its unique role, *INDEPENDENT FORCE PROTECTION: PRIVATE SECURITY FOR PREPPERS*, concentrates on addressing the latter two weaknesses inherent within other "survival" books. That is, our discussion will help you provide security to your family and friends while leading you away from military-style combat operations or excessive focus upon surviving particular crises.

Our mission here, therefore, is to keep you and your loved ones alive by avoiding confrontation, the dissemination of information, and through the elimination of those "human" characteristics that we just love to employ to shoot ourselves within the proverbial foot. You will learn that *security*, the professional concept that remains as dissimilar to the oft-compared police as it does towards the military, remains the most neglected subject by those who consider themselves "prepared" to endure any eventuality.

In our approach, we shall focus upon the following considerations:

1. Security remains a proactive subject, not a passive one despite some activities bordering upon the passive side.

2. Force protection means protecting your family and loved ones without undue consideration of local laws, legislation, and personal sensibilities.

3. The most effective security involves the least noticeable or confrontational attributes.

4. If you have to fire a gun in anger, you are *not* secure.

5. Survival means war and war means survival – anything to the contrary represents capitulation.

With these aspects in mind, we can now begin to outline our specific approach towards keeping you and your family alive, whether in your home, your 'bug out location', or anywhere in transit.

Differing, perhaps, from other books within the field, *Independent Force Protection* builds upon the following foundation:

Human life is valuable. Books on survival tend to be somewhat self-centered at best and selfish at worst. Our lives do not represent a gigantic 'King of the Hill' competition where whomever lasts the longest on earth gains the greatest prize. Rather, our efforts represent practical approaches to ensure that our loved ones and we retain a quality of life approach to the best of our abilities. That is, human beings represent *social* creatures and to forfeit community in favor of alienation does *not* represent survival – it represents thievery.

Security is survival. In its simplest definition, security represents the presence of certainty and the reduction of risk within any particular endeavor. To survive, obviously, requires certainty within your abilities and the reduction of risks against such capabilities. In this book, we shall include all activities, measures, and policies designed to defend such certainty and reduction in risks within your goal of survival.

Life evolves. Survivability represents a plan, not a diploma. That is, life is continually evolving and challenging us to either capitulate or emerge triumphant. For example, students during the 1960s learned to prepare for global nuclear warfare. Today's students *may* learn about nuclear terrorism, but few are actually taught what to do when a terrorist group detonates a nuclear or radiological device within his or her city. Similarly, individuals during the 18th century learned to survive by hunting, fishing, and combating threatening persons. During the 21st century, the focus rests more upon how to determine whether a shopper should purchase organic versus processed foods. In this regard, your individual life may span decades and what may first appear 'imminent' will appear less likely as the years ago by.

With these three 'pillars', if you will, you will begin to formulate a strategy to ensure the certainty of your life and reduce the risks associated with daily activities.

Both the process and the objective of this strategy involves the concept of *security*, which we shall include both the active ("defense") and implied ("protection") aspects of this field within this discussion. It is not, however, our intent to ensure your survival, for that rests upon you alone. Our function, within this book, is to sow the seed of self-preservation within your broader survival program. That is, we shall provide you with the knowledge required to develop, equip, and manage your personal security program, from which you shall survive to the best of your abilities and good luck.

It remains this latter concept – *luck* – that most books on survival (or other inspirational texts) fail to consider. You can represent the best, the brightest, the most experienced, and the most determined and, yet, fail miserably and often at the worst possible time. This is simply because good ideas, good intentions, and good resolve do not *always* work; you may suffer at the influence of time, others, or circumstances.

Security, therefore, represents the mitigation of uncertainty more than the elimination of challenges; more the reduction of threats than the absence of aggression. It does offer absolute protection against thieves, tyrants, and terrorists. Rather, it offers a means of defending against these malcontents in order to foster one of four possible outcomes offered by the human species: fight, flight, posture, or submission. That said, we shall not discuss the various peculiarities of the group for *fighting* remains the only survivalist mentality proposed.

Nevertheless, such "fighting" does not necessarily mean martial combat. On the contrary, fighting also means to *contend* – to struggle against or challenge. In this context, our desire to fight means not to engage within combat against armed aggressors – though that represents a strong element of life – but to fight against all those attributes that serve to distract you or prevent you from surviving throughout the day. You may fight against the climate, against the environment, against personal weaknesses, and against the progress of time. *That*, folks, is what security is all about.

Are you *ready*?

RECOMMENDED READINGS

Balor, P. (1988). *Manual of the Mercenary Soldier*. Boulder: Paladin Press.

Bodansky, Y. (1994). *TERROR! The inside story of the terrorist conspiracy in America*. SPI Books.

Bodansky, Y. (2007). *Chechen Jihad: Al-Qaeda's Training Ground and the Next Wave of Terror*. New York: Harper.

Bowden, M. (2001). *Killing Pablo: The Hunt for the World's Greatest Outlaw*. New York: Penguin Books.

Brands, H. (2009). *Mexico's Narco-Insurgency and U.S. Counterdrug Policy*. Carlisle, PA: Strategic Studies Institute.

Cwiek, M. A. (2005). America after 9/11. In G. R. Ledlow, J. A. Johnson, & W. J. Jones (Eds.), *Community Preparedness and Response to Terrorism: The Terrorist Threat and Community Response* (Vol. I, pp. 7-21). Westport, Connecticut: Praeger.

Dzikansky, M., Kleiman, G., & Slater, R. (2012). *Terrorist Suicide Bombings: Attack Interdiction, Mitigation, and Response*. Boca Raton, FL: CRC Press.

Emerson, S. (2002). *American Jihad: The Terrorists Living Amongst Us*. New York: The Free Press.

Gray, C. S. (2006). *Another Bloody Century: Future Warfare*. London: Phoenix.

Hamilton, S. (2009, November). Cyber Threats: We don't know what we don't know. *Armed Forces Journal*, pp. 33-34, 41.

Kan, P. R. (2008). *Drug Intoxicated Irregular Fighters: Complications, Dangers, and Responses*. Carlisle, PA: Strategic Studies Institute.

Kan, P. R. (2011). *Mexico's "Narco-Refugees": The Looming Challenge for U.S. National Security*. Carlisle, PA: Strategic Studies Institute.

Kellner, T., & Pipitone, F. (2010). Inside Mexico's Drug War. *World Policy Journal*, 29-37.

Martines, L. (2012). Mexican Crime Cartels. *Journal of Counterterrorism & Homeland Security International, 18*(1), 36-40.

Norell, J. O. (September). Are you an American or Are you a Terrorist? *America's 1st Freedom*, pp. 30-33, 56-57.

O'Neill, B. E. (1978). *Armed Struggle in Palestine: A Political-Military Analysis*. Boulder: Westview Press.

Spicer, M. (2011). Mexican Drug Cartels: The Growing Threat of the Sniper Attack. *Journal of Counterterrorism & Homeland Security International, 16*(4), 48-50.

United States Department of Homeland Security. (2008). *Terrorist Weaponization of Fire: Improvised Incendiary Devices (IID) and Arson*. Transportation Security Administration, Office of Intelligence. Washington: U.S. Government.

TO SURVIVE

TO SURVIVE MEANS that you will undertake every conceivable effort to endure, no matter the challenge or the obstacle. Furthermore, you will devote your *entire* existence – not merely a few hours, a work shift, or an academic course – to the process. It does not represent something that you like to do or even how you prefer to do it. Surviving means doing everything that you need to do whenever you need to do it and under the best possible effort for the conditions that you experience at that time. In other words, survival is not a chance nor is failure an option if you wish to arise again another day.

Too much popularity has been spent on the notion of one being a prepper or a survivalist as if these personalities are somehow new and original. If they seem this way, it is only because people have forgotten how to *live* – not that they are afraid of dying. Our modern, convenience-laden society has taken the guesswork away from how to eat, how to drink, how to clothe oneself, and how to build shelter. What was once common domestic responsibilities has simply turned into uncommon "rebellion" amongst those that prefer not to allow his or her cell phone do the navigating or their car to parallel park for them (some of us, after all, have been known to read maps or parallel park tractor-trailer rigs).

Listen, *everyone* is terrified of dying. Yes, a few homicide bombers and shooters actually go out and seek death, but this is primarily because they are also afraid of *living*. Their actions result because his or her mind suggests that the fear of dying is less terrible than the fear that "hope" is not offered from the other side. In other words, they escape from this world to the next because he or she cannot accept the conditions under which they live during the present. Therefore, do not believe *anyone* that says that he or she is not afraid of dying. Most of us, however, are even more afraid of *how* we die.

For the sake of discussion, for example, you are hereby given a choice in dying. Either you will be locked within a cage, doused with gasoline, and lit afire *or* you will die peacefully at 120 years old surrounded by friends and family. Which would *you* prefer? Naturally, we have now come to the realization that dying was not as fearful as the thought of dying *horribly*. All of us, it can be surmised, prefer to die in the exact same way: *unexpectedly, of extreme old age*.

Unfortunately for the world, there remains a sizeable portion of the population – as much as sixty-five percent, if Dr. Stanley Milgram's Yale University studies during the 1960s continue to be supported by subsequent research – that prevents us from such expectations. In fact, we have *all* known people that, for various reasons, died during his or her relative youth. It may involve injury, disease, crime, or freak accident, but these unfortunate individuals did not stand a chance of dying at a ripe old age.

Ours, therefore, is a desire or perhaps even *want* to survive into extreme old age. None of us ever, with good conscience, *expects* to survive. There are a great many professional sports teams that expect to win championships but fail miserably when confronting smaller, less talented and less paid teams that obviously wanted to win more. Mere money and individual accomplishments do not provide much to the 'team' and your own survival undoubtedly bears itself upon the shoulders of a great many other individuals.

To survive, you must continuously strive for longevity without ever falling victim to that sinister confidence that arises once we have concluded that we have achieved our objective – that we *expect* to survive simply because we have stored all the right supplies, read the best books, and learned to handle every form of weapon under the sun. What happens, for instance, if we slip on a rock and crash down into a crevice? Or, for that matter, what happens if we suffer a stroke from an undiagnosed condition and are left forever bedridden?

Every "survivalist" on the planet could literally climb out of such crevices by walking upon the books of knowledge that he or she has failed to consider. This is just human nature. As with political pundits, few realize that he or she does not know *everything*. Frankly, this is one of the reasons why this "prepper" book strives to be different from all the other books that you have undoubtedly read. Far too many people on this planet remain too full of themselves to make a difference; they do not believe that they can learn anything new so do not even bother trying.

You, on the other hand, represent a knowledge sponge or, rather, an information curator. You like to collect information from the widest possible sources, catalog it away within your brain, and retrieve it whenever the need arises. You do not care much about from *where* you learned this information; just that it *could be useful* at some point in the future. You read not only non-fiction books, but fiction novels as well for the creative spirit of the author represents just such an innovative mind as is needed to provide you with a solution. You look at household objects and "remanufacture" them within your mind to serve other uses. You are, therefore, a *survivor*.

Yours is a life predicted upon the five dictums of survival:

1. ***It's not over until it's over.*** You represent a human being, which means that you can manipulate both your environment and your circumstances within it when compared with other animal species. Biblical Samson killed one thousand Philistines with the jawbone of an ass because he knew that even a bone could be turned into an instrument of survival. How many people starve to death today because they cannot see past the packaging and schedules to realize that food does not always come from the grocery store shelf or that a person can survive on less than three meals per day. As long as you possess a heartbeat, you have a chance to live.

2. ***Who cares where it came from?*** Were you aware that one of the most prized furs on the market is neither mink nor sable, but *skunk*? Some of the most nutritious substances on the planet bear the most regrettable of tastes and odors (which is probably a defense mechanism against being eaten). Furthermore, any government or international body does not regulate some of the deadliest weapons on the planet. When you embark upon your life as a survivalist, you begin with a clean slate where race, wealth, gender, education, and physical abilities matter little – providing that you are able to make use of what exist all around you irrespective of prejudices.

3. ***Things happen.*** It never fails; you build a survival bungalow able to withstand a 35-kiloton nuclear bomb and the first thing that happens is that a meteorite pummels your dream abode into the ground. Well, we have yet to hear this happen, but the story does suggest that strange things happen even to the prepared. For this reason, one can never be secure in the knowledge that he or she has considered every available contingency. Things just happen

that befuddle both scientists and theologians. You must possess a sense of humor and a friendly perspective about life (watch the ending of *The Treasure of the Sierra Madre* for a valuable clue). There will be days when your best-laid plans crumble all around you and you begin to wonder if some ancestral goat pissed into the village witch's caldron for such things to happen. Be that as it may, things just happen within life and these unfortunate events provide *meaning* to survival.

4. ***Fitness does not really matter.*** Ever notice toned 'Gym Queens' on a long hike through the mountains? Even with six-pack abs and huge biceps, they quickly lose energy and breath on these trips because for all of their pumping iron, they have not retained enough body fat to store energy. Conversely, a somewhat flabby middle-aged individual is likely to walk on forever without tiring. Sure, he is not as "strong" as the bodybuilder is, but strength comes in various forms and remains quite subjective. This, of course, is not to say that an obese person is likely to survive. You still need sufficient strength to move your person through dangerous terrain; just not to the point where you sacrifice your energy for a bit more lifting power.

5. ***Spirituality is not a sin.*** Too many people think that they can do everything for him or herself. More pronounced is the belief that people represent the pantheon of existence. Actually, we represent the reason for *Creation* – but not the *cause* of creation. Saint Simeon Stylites (390?-459 A.D.), for instance, lived atop a sixty-foot pillar no larger than your toilet *uninterruptedly* for three decades. The rope that tied him to the pillar was absorbed into his body by his flesh after those great many years and offered maggots a chance to feast. Nevertheless, Saint Simeon replaced the maggots that had fallen from his body so that they would not, in turn, starve to death. That he and his followers – some of which lived on ever-taller perches for upwards of sixty years! – accomplished such a remarkable feat had little to do with muscles or knowledge. They simply believed that that was the kind of life that God intended for them to have. From this perspective, your own survival within the wilderness would prove to be extremely easy. You just need to believe that your survival rests within the hands of "something" a bit stronger, more compassionate, and definitely more caring than you care to admit.

From these five rules, we can begin to understand how easy it may be to survive. All that it takes is to relinquish your hold on what is expected or preferable and focus upon those attributes that bear a fundamental role in your success whenever faced with challenges. In other words, success is relatively simple if we consider it an intangible objective. On the other hand, if we set rigid goals, then it can be extremely difficult to achieve.

We are, of course, speaking about the mental aspects rather than the physical ones, for eating a dead squirrel, as an example, remains less troubling than merely considering the option. When a person is hungry enough, they will eat *anything*. This is true with a great many things as, for instance, those new to the military often discover that he or she can sleep anywhere and during any time of the day – such represents the preciousness of the nap in front of him or her in context with the sheer exhaustion that every military veteran encounters at some point.

To borrow a line, success equals effort plus resilience plus knowledge plus common sense plus luck – not all of which are in surplus today. At least appreciated by the average person, specifically resilience and luck. Few want to exert the former and no one wants to consider the latter as we all want the greatest degree of success through the least troubling circumstances. After all, no one wants to blow the championship game on dumb luck. Yet, many do. And those that fail the worst do not ever take into account such improbable results.

If we conclude that survival represents long-term planning for short-term challenges, then we must not be too carried away with planning for things that we are unlikely to confront. For instance, New York City residents would do well to avoid planning over volcanic eruptions. The same as with residents of Honolulu preparing for blizzard activity. On the other hand, both would benefit to consider muggings, riots, and other criminal activities as potential threats.

Table 1. Representative Threats

	City	Rural	Coastal
Hurricane	X	?	X
Earthquake	X	X	X
Crime	X	?	X
Terrorism	X	?	X

Table 1 briefly shows comparative threats for cities, rural communities, and coastal areas. With a large portion of the human population residing near the coastline, such environments share the same potentialities as urban areas. Nevertheless, rural areas do not escape these threats; rather, they are reduced in proportion to the size and location of that particular community. What this suggests is that survivalists and preppers cannot dismiss any but the most extreme of threat possibilities.

With this preliminary description of survival and common sense in mind, the conscientious individual may now turn to the basis for this book – the inherent challenge for all persons planning and *wanting* to survive the next "unexpected" catastrophe – however it may be termed or categorized.

RECOMMENDED READINGS

Balor, P. (1988). *Manual of the Mercenary Soldier.* Boulder: Paladin Press

Couch, D. (2010). *A Tactical Ethic: Moral Conduct in the Insurgent Battlespace.* Annapolis, MD: Naval Institute Press.

Dewar, M. (1992). *War in the Streets: The Story of Urban Combat from Calais to Khafji.* London: David & Charles.

England, J. W. (1987). *Long-Range Patrol Operations: Reconnaissance, Combat, and Special Operations.* Boulder: Paladin Press.

Gander, T. (1990). *Guerrilla Warfare Weapons: The Modern Underground Fighter's Armoury.* New York: Sterling Publishing Co., Inc.

Godlewski, R. (2009). Human Intelligence: Perceiving an Enemy's Thoughts. *American Intelligence Journal, 27*(1), 29-37.

Grossman, D. (2009). *On Killing: The Psychological Cost of Learning to Kill in War and Society* (Revised ed.). New York: Back Bay Books.

Hurth, J. D. (2012). *Combat Tracking Guide.* Mechanicsburg, PA: Stackpole Books.

Kan, P. R. (2008). *Drug Intoxicated Irregular Fighters: Complications, Dangers, and Responses.* Carlisle, PA: Strategic Studies Institute.

Lawrence, E. (2005). *Tactical Pistol Shooting.* Iola, WI: Gun Digest Books.

Lung, H. (2006). *Mind Control: The Ancient Art of Psychological Warfare.* New York: Citadel Press.

Machine, G. (2011). *Israeli Security Warrior Training.* Boulder: Paladin Press.

McRaven, W. H. (1996). *SPEC OPS: Case Studies in Special Operations Warfare: Theory and Practice.* New York: Ballantine Books.

Sockut, E. (1995). *Secrets of Street Survival -- Israeli Style: Staying alive in a Civilian War Zone.* Boulder: Paladin Press.

BREAKDOWN OF SOCIETY

NOT TOO LONG ago, at a large national retailer in Arkansas, the company decided to have a three-day going out of business sale for a local store that it decided to close forever. In a spat of questionable brilliance, the retail giant decided to state "Everything *must* go!" hoping to stimulate a last minute spike in sales, presumably to avoid transporting away hundreds of unsold products. In less than two days, aggressive shoppers had hauled away *everything* not nailed down – and, perhaps, a few items that were – in what amounted to a looting free-for-all. Shelves, security cameras, building materials, *everything* within the walls of that store had disappeared under the pretext of bargain shopping.

What this teaches us about people is that a great many of us will turn to looting and rioting at the least provocation. It does not even have to be a major catastrophe as the above referenced sale – in a relatively peaceful town of "only" 40,000 residents – suggests. If blood was shed over saving a few dollars at a store that obviously could not make any money in order to stay put in the first place, just imagine what will happen when food and water are scare. If people were injured simply because a "sale" sign was placed upon a store window, just imagine what will happen when starving and ill-prepared masses learn that *your* home contains food, medicine, and firearms – not to mention your teenage daughter.

To defend against such crises, your survival rests upon two distinct fields that you may have not considered or have ill-conceived notions about: *intelligence* and *security*. We shall discuss these two fields within subsequent chapters. For now, however, we must relate to how they fit in with the breakdown of society as rioters, looters, and other opportunists tear about your community whether you live within the city, a rural farmland environment, or on the coast.

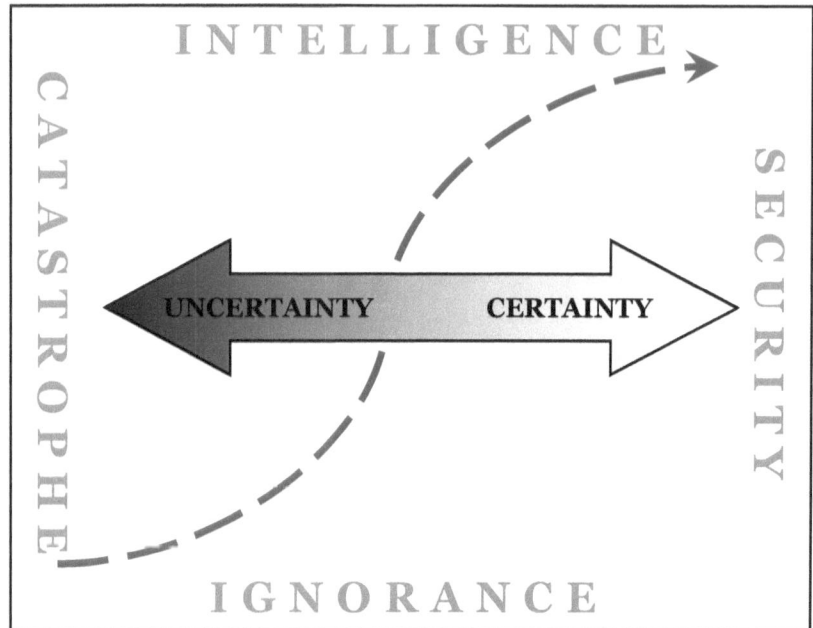

Figure 1. Relationship between intelligence and security.

In Figure 1, we can ascertain the relationship between security and intelligence. With more intelligence – that is, *actionable* information – the further an individual moves away from ignorance and towards security. This, in turn, promotes certainty that enables that individual to move away from catastrophe (in the sense that such events remain largely chaotic). For its role, however, intelligence means far more than merely the acquisition and accumulation of knowledge. It can be considered that information that allows an individual or group to achieve a *decided advantage* over an adversary.

Ignored by most people, however, represents the concept of *counterintelligence* – those activities and policies undertaken to keep useful information *away* from the thoughts and actions of adversaries. This represents basic Sun Tzu logic: to know your enemy and yourself (and, by extension, preventing him from knowing you). If you are smart – that is, *aware* – and he or she is ignorant, you can plan your functions more profitably. This is why professional football teams, for instance, go to extraordinary lengths to keep their "trick play" practices secret.

Returning to our analysis of societal breakdown, such things do *not* appear within a vacuum. The infamous case of the 1999 "Battle of Seattle" warrants a brief discussion. This event arose during the meeting of the World Trade Organization (WTO) that pitted globalization against anti-trade activists. Two principal groups were known to target the meeting – the Direct Action Network (DAN) and labor unions. Both remained concerned over the shift in jobs to undeveloped nations and the perceived exploitation thereof. The Seattle Police determined that its best hope in maintaining order was to support the labor march and hope that its presence would draw in DAN supporters, and the combined mass would move safely away from the WTO to a location where the labor rally would be held.

Unfortunately, in among the labor and activist groups lurked the even more sinister organization known as the Black Bloc – anarchists that simply wanted to disrupt society. This group succeeded in destroying any semblance to law and order and the WTO event ended in a city in chaos and several prominent municipal and police officials out of a job. If you live within or near a large city, you would do well to analyze this signature event for its study outlines several prominent lessons for survivalists and preppers to consider.

Our intention here, however, is to suggest that the lack of intelligence led to this disaster. The Seattle Police simply had no way of knowing how many protestors there would be within the city and how they would react. Furthermore, the police officials in charge of "security" – again, a field *not* akin to law enforcement – erroneously assumed that one group of protestors (the labor unions) could handle another (the anti-globalization activists). This violates the first law of human physics – crowds grow unstable with more divergent additions; the Black Bloc anarchists were able to sway members of the DAN affiliated groups to go astray, leading to the inability of the union protestors to corral the crowds.

Despite many prepper and survivalist individuals believing in fantastical 'end of the world' scenarios, the concerns for general breakdowns in society remain much smaller – and localized. The Los Angeles, Baltimore, and Ferguson, Missouri riots are just a few examples of urban destruction committed during the past quarter-century. *All* these incidents, however, involved perceived injustices against black individuals by police officers. The trend, therefore, suggests that *any* confrontation between blacks and police officers bears a high potential for urban collapse. These three examples – suggesting where police *did* act inappropriately, *may* have acted inappropriately, and did *not* act inappropriately – illustrate the ineffectiveness of dialogue. People that *wish* to destroy, *will* destroy regardless of justification.

This bears significant implications for you and your families, for ultimately you have to move through such urban centers, as few people are able to avoid their presence during the course of time. To survive within

such an environment requires that you consciously understand how
societies break down. Do large segments of the population flow together in
unison to affect some grievance? Or do small segments of the population,
as with Seattle during 1999, take advantage of grievances to instill their
wider ambitions.

**Figure 2. Bootleg copy of Carlos Marighella's book on urban
warfare.** © Unknown.

Figure 2 illustrates a copy of Carlos Marighella's *Mini-Manual of
Urban Guerrilla Warfare* produced during the late 1960s or early 1970s by
elements of the Weather Underground or Black Panther movement in
Chicago. This book, however, contains a great deal more than just

Marighella's Latin American manifesto on fighting guerrilla warfare within the city.

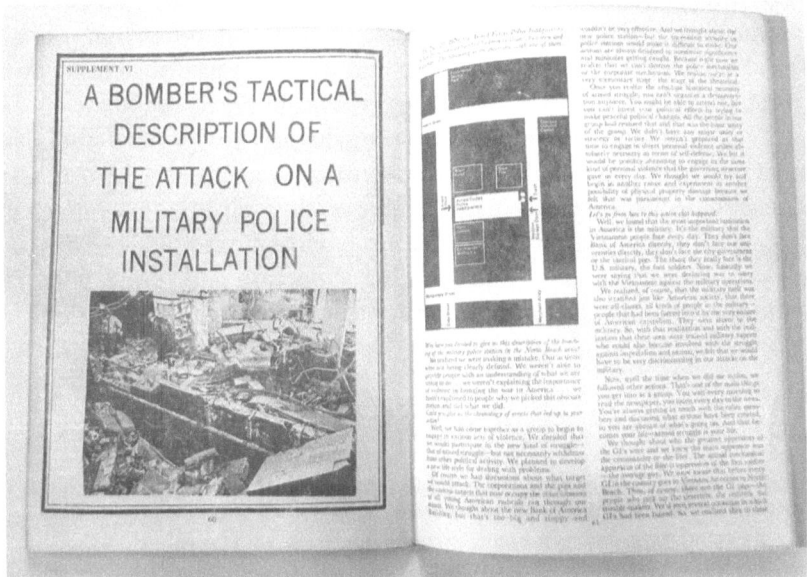

Figure 3. Addendum to Marighella's text on Urban Guerrilla warfare, dealing with attacks on military police stations. © Unknown.

In Figure 3, we see an addendum included within the booklet depicted in Figure 2, which deals specifically with the attack upon a military police station. From this, we can deduce that radical elements within America's heartland drew interest in attacking both military *and* law enforcement targets. In other words, these criminal organizations were preparing to attack any semblance of law and order within the United States. That this publication was printed decades ago cannot be discounted. In fact, the anti-police elements within the United States appear even more pronounced during the present (2015) and, therefore, offer concerned citizens greater threats to consider.

Given this reality, the collapse of any particular society – herein usually referred to as communities as global or national shattering calamities will severely affect *anyone's* ability to survive – must remain at the front of any prepper or survivalist's mind. These situations fester for long periods before they finally erupt; normally peaceful and content communities do not decide one moment from the next whether they are going to riot and loot. That retailer in Arkansas did *not* create the environment in which thousands of local residents decided to act as if insurgents. Rather, the "sale" simply served as the spark that ignited the conflagration that simmered beneath the surface. Were the residents eagerly awaiting a store to destroy? Did they perceive themselves as economically disadvantaged and therefore sought *any opportunity* to gain material advantage? Were they people that were merely drawn away by the destructive behavior of other malcontents? We simply do not know.

To bear any chance of determining the psychology of an underlying population requires us to delve deeper into intelligence and, by extension, counterintelligence. Your security depends exclusively upon how much you know about your community and your environment coupled with how much you can *keep* others from knowing about you and your family. This latter aspect remains the most important element, but first things first.

RECOMMENDED READINGS

AbuKhalil, A. (2005). Arab-Israeli Conflict. In C. Press, *The Middle East* (Tenth Edition ed., pp. 13-78). Washington: CQ Press.

Benson, R. (1986). *Gunrunning for Fun & Profit*. Boulder: Paladin Press.

Brands, H. (2009). *Mexico's Narco-Insurgency and U.S. Counterdrug Policy*. Carlisle, PA: Strategic Studies Institute.

Byman, D. (2005). *Deadly Connections: States that Sponsor Terrorism*. New York: Cambridge University Press.

Kahaner, L. (2007). *AK-47: The weapon that changed the face of war*. Hoboken: John Wiley & Sons, Inc.

Kan, P. R. (2011). *Mexico's "Narco-Refugees": The Looming Challenge for U.S. National Security*. Carlisle, PA: Strategic Studies Institute.

Kellner, T., & Pipitone, F. (2010). Inside Mexico's Drug War. *World Policy Journal*, 29-37.

Khosrokhavar, F. (2005). *Suicide Bombers: Allah's New Martyrs*. London: Pluto Press.

Lee, G. D. (2004). *Global Drug Enforcement: Practical Investigative Techniques*. Boca Raton, FL: CRC Press.

McMains, M. J., & Mullins, W. C. (2010). *Crisis Negotiations: Managing Critical Incidents and Hostage Situations in Law Enforcement and Corrections* (4th ed.). New Providence, NJ: Matthew Bender & Company.

Oatman, R. L. (2006). *Executive Protection: New Solutions for a New Era*. Arnold, Maryland: Noble House.

Phalen, D. (2011). Protecting Those Who Save Lives. *The Journal of Counterterrorism & Homeland Security International, 17*(2), 24-26.

Rehov, P. (Producer), & Rehov, P. (Director). (2006). [Motion Picture].

Sloan, S., & Bunker, R. J. (2011). *Red Teams and Counterterrorism Training*. Norman, OK: University of Oklahoma Press.

Sperry, P. (2005). *Infiltration: How Muslim Spies and Subversives have Penetrated Washington*. Nashville: Nelson Current.

Stojkovic, S., Kalinich, D., & Klofas, J. (2012). *Criminal Justice Organizations: Administration and Management* (Fifth Edition ed.). Belmont, CA: Wadsworth.

INTELLIGENCE

NO INDIVIDUAL CAN plan without knowing what he or she intends to accomplish. No individual can perceive without understanding the nature of human senses. Finally, no individual can process knowledge without understanding how to attach value to seemingly inconsequential bits of information. These represent the field of intelligence, the process of gaining strategic and tactical advantage through the proper utilization of actionable information.

To understand the concept of information versus intelligence, we can employ some rather simple examples:

Table 2. Comparisons between information and intelligence.

INFORMATION	INTELLIGENCE
You learn that a new boy is coming to take your teenage daughter to the movies.	You learn that the new boy coming to take your teenage daughter to the movies was recently arrested on drunken driving charges.
A new car salesperson tells you that the latest model sedan is *just* the car for you and can offer you a great interest rate.	You discover that the car being pitched to you has had significant recalls in the past *and* your FICO score is well below the requirement for tier 1 interest rates.
A neighbor remarks that the sky "looks like rain" heading your way.	You observe on the NOAA Website radar a massive storm heading in your direction.
A local mayor says that your town is peaceful and secure.	You learn that local police reserves are being activated for undisclosed reasons.

We can determine from the scenarios offer in Table 2 that information is just that, *information* provided without much context. *Intelligence*, to the contrary, leads to advantage on your part. In the first example, simply knowing that a boy is coming to pick up your daughter does not imply concern one way or another. On the other hand, knowing that this particular boy had been arrested for drunken driving *does* offer you a distinct opportunity to *judge* (as would be the case if the boy turned out to be a marvelous representative of society). In the second case, your knowledge about the automobile *plus* your review of your own credit report means that you understand that, despite the salesperson's pitch, you would be paying too much for a car that holds little promises for successful operation. The car *may* have the bugs worked out and the dealer *may* still be able to offer you a great interest rate, but the advantage nevertheless lies in your favor.

The third example offers a perspective on human intelligence (HUMINT). Your neighbor *is*, after all, providing you with accurate information. That is, rain *is* heading your way. He or she may be someone that you trust immeasurably and, therefore, no further verification is required. That said, the use of the Internet to actually see the storms encroaching upon your location removes any *doubt* about your chances. It is the same as with seeing smoke within your home. Such a sighting may not be bad; sometimes, for instance, food particles on a stove's burner will produce smoke. On the other hand, actually sighting *fire* warrants a more proactive effort on your part (even if the flames merely erupt from your stove's burner).

The final example warrants deeper reflection and builds upon the above. If your mayor is trustworthy, then it is no big deal. The same as with the police reserves being activated with no apparent reason. They may be on training missions. There may be a parade or sporting event nearby that requires extra labor. What the activation requires, however, is a bit of investigation on your part. A politician may say whatever he or she pleases, but physical activity – especially on the part of the law enforcement community – warrants further inspection. Such a scenario may involve nothing more than the weekly college football game, but what happens if your team loses (or wins for that matter)? Rowdy college students have been known to literally burn down towns with the least provocation.

The trick involving information or intelligence rests with your own plan for survival. In other words, *you* bear the responsibility for determining whether any bit of information is of actionable value to you or not. You cannot rely upon others to decide this for you. For instance, in the first example above, if you had a son that was going to pick up a girl that was recently arrested for drunken driving, you may not be as worried because, presumably, your son would be a safe and reliable driver that *would not drink.* In this case, we are discussing, essentially, the exact same information, but now it holds little valuable for your concerns about your child.

Deciphering intelligence requires one to play around with scraps of information, perhaps toss them about your mind while you are driving home from work or eating lunch, and then seeing if "something" materializes that brings solution or success to your specific needs. A good analogy has always been to think of obtaining actionable information as assembling two jigsaw puzzles from a combined heap with little more to go on than a rough sketch of what each individual puzzle is suppose to look like.

To aid within your determinations whether something exists as intelligence or mere "information", the following considerations should be reviewed:

- ***What is the problem that confronts you immediately?*** Yours is a goal to survive for as long as possible but, again, each day brings its own challenges. Therefore, you must focus on your day-to-day objectives while keeping the future in reserve (if you cannot survive today, you will not possess a future anyway). Is your function to arrive home from a trip safely? To secure a source of water and food? To reach your bug out location? Each of these requirements possesses different needs and obligations with a unique series of challenges to confront.

- ***What types of information could benefit you the most?*** Even without knowing sources, you retain a need to know for most events. For instance, in determining whether you will return from home safely, you may need to know airline schedules, traffic conditions, weather, etc. – things that stand in your way of going from Point A to Point B. On the other hand, if you were traveling to your 'bug out location', you may need to include information regarding potential hazards, what, precisely, is the reason for your bail out of your nice comfortable home, etc. Unless you have no clue as to what challenges you are likely to face, you will know what types of information are more valuable than others are. For instance, knowing that Interstate-75 is closed down due to an accident places you at great advantage over those that are not aware of this and will clutter the highway through his or her ignorance.

- ***From what sources are you best served by?*** *All* sources of information can be considered to be biased. If you purchase a new automobile, for instance, any information that you receive from the dealer, friends, technical publications, etc. are influenced by the motives of that particular group. If you ride with a Chevrolet enthusiast, for example, he or she may point out every Ford or Chrysler that is broken down along the highway. A visitor from Europe may equate America's rampant crime, not with freedom to act, but with the availability of firearms. A religious fundamentalist for his or her role may attribute "bad luck" to a person's offenses against God. The list could go on. Knowing this, you must actually perform intelligence functions against your intelligence sources. That is, you must question the motives of *everyone* or every source of information that you retrieve to see if that information may be verified by an independent source. For instance, if your Chevy-loving friend complains about Fords, verify their statements with recall records, longevity of the automobiles, and repeat buyers. Simply going with, say, sales numbers may only mean that Ford bears more marketing savvy than Chevrolet. Suspect *everything*.

- ***How are you likely to be influenced by the information?*** Sometimes intelligence appears that you had not considered previously. For example, regarding the third scenario in Table 2. Let us say that you had a bad day at work and hurried home to take a brief ride on that brand new Harley-Davidson motorcycle that you had just dropped $40,000 on. In your haste to go riding, you ignored to consider the weather. Your neighbor's offhand remark about a storm on the horizon may keep you from getting soaked and ruining your "bad day" even further. In this case, this casual piece of information – that you had heretofore not considered to be of value – now provides you with a certain advantage (that of not getting wet). Since you may not have considered many thoughts beforehand, you must learn to analyze *all* information that flows into your mind. This takes practice and experience, but sooner or later separating intelligence from basic information will become second nature.

With intelligence thus perceived, it become easier to plan your daily and weekly functions.

To aid within these endeavors, you must begin to *categorize* the intelligence that you will begin to accumulate. Simply separating actionable intelligence from information only represents part of the intelligence collection process. You must classify all intelligence so that you will be able to both recall the information when required *and* pair it with other data. For the purposes of our discussion, we can group intelligence into three categories: white, yellow, and red – depending upon the criticality of the information possessed:

White Intelligence: Most information represents that which you gather everyday of your life. It represents mere static; information that holds little value to your life one way or another. It is retained simply because your mind does not forget much of anything (even if your conscious mind rarely recalls it). Nevertheless, certain tidbits of knowledge surface as intriguing, such as when you learn of a new product or a new way of doing something. You perceive of some value in this data, but, as of yet, it does not influence any activity that you engage within.

Yellow Intelligence: On occasion, you will determine that some information bears merit within your life, such as the aforementioned scenario of rain affecting your transformation into biker. Naturally, of course, it may *not* have rained, but the mere threat kept you from undertaking an activity. The same rests with the scenario involving the boy arrested for drunken driving escorting your daughter on a date. By itself, there is nothing to suggest that his previous escapade would have irreparably harmed your daughter. Nevertheless, the mere suspicion of his poor living and driving habits kept you from taking the chance. These incidences represent 'yellow intelligence' information that causes you to avoid taking chances just to be safe. In other words, it may never rain, but you still take the umbrella to work. Similarly, you may never have been robbed in your entire life, yet you still lock your doors at night because *others have been robbed.*

Red Intelligence. Eventually, information becomes critical – a potential for life or death. You may have heard that a tornado is bearing down upon your location or that an active shooter has appeared within your place of work. Regardless, such information warrants that you become *proactive* rather than merely alert. Upon receiving category red intelligence, you simply cease what you are doing and proceed into defense mode. To the best of your ability, you *must* possess a plan of action for every conceivable eventuality for upon receiving red intelligence, you may have literally seconds to act.

Too often, as with the case of the U.S. Department of Homeland Security (DHS), agencies and groups try to overcomplicate the categorization of knowledge or response. Many tactical firearms instructors, for instance, employ Jeff Cooper's White-Yellow-Orange-Red code of awareness, but this simply adds an additional layer of function. Since your function remains to survive under a range of conditions, your intelligence acquisition – as miniscule as it is when compared with agencies such as the CIA, FBI, etc. – merely needs to keep you calm, alert, or active as the threat may be.

From here, we can now turn the discussion to *counterintelligence* for the simple reason that knowing about threats does little if you do not shield knowledge about *you* from prying eyes. We have all seen incidences in which people volunteer far too much information about him or her or their family. Such examples include:

- Parents that proudly display 'Honor Student' bumper stickers on their cars. This provides criminals with an opportunity to determine who has young children within their households, which schools they attend, and, most especially, what type of vehicle that you drive to pick up those children.

- Shoppers that sign up for retailer discount cards. This provides the company with a range of information about your buying habits, such as what products that you purchase, when you purchase them, and what payment types (e.g., checking accounts, credit cards, etc.) that you use. You may not be able to keep this information private once it is out of your hands.

- Individuals post too much information about themselves online. It remains incredulous how many people will post every little detail about him or herself (and about their families) on such sites as Facebook, MySpace, YouTube, etc. This information becomes *permanent* owing to the nature of the Internet and allows criminals and terrorists to deduce much information about you, your home life, and your employer.

If the concept of counterintelligence exists to keep others from knowing about it, then it remains common sense to avoid *giving* information to them willingly.

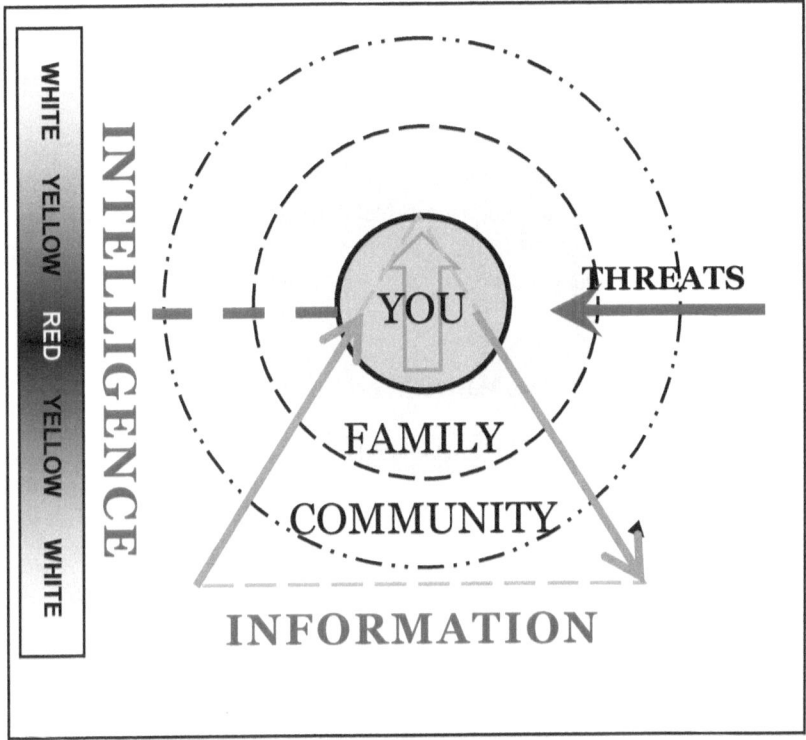

Figure 4. The world of counterintelligence.

In Figure 4, we can see the relationship between intelligence, information, threats, and security. Criminals and terrorists can detect the information flow between you, your family, and the outside community (the entire planet in today's age of globalization and the Internet). These threats can use your community and family, in turn, to target you, which elevates your intelligence level from white to yellow and finally to red as threats zero in on your person. This requires your efforts to impose information "discipline" upon your family, though you shall remain subject to your broader community. For this reason, it remains imperative that you avoid compromising yourself by freely giving out information of value to outside parties.

From another perspective, you must refrain from activities that draw attention to you – no flashy red Camaro or decked out Harley-Davidson. *Anything* that stands out from the crowd will immediately be noticed by virtually anyone within eyesight. Driving a fancy automobile, for example, will imply "wealth" to someone seeking to profit from your loss. To engage within counterintelligence effectively, you must begin to scrutinize your environment from an outsider's perspective and see if you can detect anything that may make you a more attractive target to potential threats.

With a proper plan in place to obtain actionable information about your community and the world, coupled with a discreet program to evaluate how to keep you and your family from becoming broadly known to that global community, you can now begin an effective security operation to keep yourself surviving well into the future.

RECOMMENDED READINGS

Bodansky, Y. (2007). *Chechen Jihad: Al-Qaeda's Training Ground and the Next Wave of Terror*. New York: Harper.

Cragin, K., & Hoffman, B. (2003). *Arms Trafficking and Colombia*. Santa Monica, CA: RAND Corporation.

Ellis, J. W. (2007). *Police Analysis and Planning for Homicide Bombings: Prevention, Defense, and Response*. Springfield, IL: Charles C. Thomas Publisher, Ltd.

Gabriel, M. A. (2006). *Journey into the Mind of an Islamic Terrorist*. Lake Mary, Florida: Front Line.

Jaber, H. (1997). *Hezbollah: Born with a Vengeance*. New York: Columbia University Press.

Jones, A., Kovacich, G. l., & Luzwick, P. G. (2002). *Global Information Warfare: How Businesses, Governments, and Others Achieve Objectives and Attain Competitive Advantages*. New York: Auerbach.

Magee, A. C. (2009, Winter). Counterintelligence in Irregular Warfare: A Void in the Full-Spectrum Joint Force Capability. *American Intelligence Journal*, pp. 54-60.

McRaven, W. H. (1996). *SPEC OPS: Case Studies in Special Operations Warfare: Theory and Practice*. New York: Ballantine Books.

Miller, C. R. (2005). *Electromagnetic Pulse Threats in 2010*. Maxwell AFB: Center for Strategy and Technology, Air War College/Air University.

Nance, M. W. (2014). *Terrorist Recognition Handbook: A Practitioner's Manual for Predicting and Indentifying Terrorist Activities* (Third ed.). Boca Raton, FL: CRC Press.

Paladin Press. (1991). *Federal Bomb Intelligence: U.S. Government Guide to Terrorist Explosives*. Boulder: Paladin Press.

Sloan, S., & Bunker, R. J. (2011). *Red Teams and Counterterrorism Training*. Norman, OK: University of Oklahoma Press.

Smith, J. (2009). *A Law Enforcement and Security Officers' Guide to Responding to Bomb Threats* (Second ed.). Springfield, IL: Charles C. Thomas.

Steele, R. D. (2010). *Human Intelligence: All Humans, All Minds, All the Time*. Carlisle, PA: Strategic Studies Institute.

Thurman, J. T. (2006). *Practical Bomb Scene Investigation*. Boca Raton, FL: CRC Press.

SECURITY

THE ESSENCE OF security remains to keep you, your family, and your immediate environment safe from threat and your actions functioning with a fair degree of certainty. Under this broad definition rests two distinct but cooperative disciplines: protection and defense. For the purposes of this book, we shall categorize these fields under the following interpretations:

> *Protection*: Passive activities undertaken to provide care and comfort to persons or properties that may find themselves under potential threat from artificial or natural crises.

> *Defense*: Active measures undertaken to deter or respond to threats (primarily human) targeting persons or properties under one's care.

With these basic definitions in mind, we can discuss a few examples of both terms.

First, an individual installing a security system within his or her home is providing *protection* for the individuals residing within that home. This alarm system may not actually defend these persons, but its presence does offer a degree of comfort and certainty for family members. Another form of protection involves unarmed security guards roaming a local mall. These employees, in and of themselves, could not stop aggression, but their presence does offer comfort to shoppers who may need to be directed to safer areas under certain crises. Protection could also mean acquiring flood insurance for those citizens that live near a major river prone to breaking its high-water levels during the rainy season. The homeowner may still lose a great deal, but the policy provides peace of mind should they need to rebuild or replace some assets.

The concept of *defense*, conversely, implies a great deal of activity that exceeds mere protection. It may mean something as simple as placing sandbags around one's house to deter encroaching water. You are, after all, defending a home from an aggressive river. Yet, not all deterrence issues provide peace of mind. For instance, let us say that you had recently defended your home against an intruder and were thus forced to kill that burglar because he pulled a gun on you. Very few people would find comfort with the aftermath of such a traumatic event even if those under your care were foremost within your mind.

Communities may also have to defend themselves against rioters, which means that concerned citizens may rise in support of local law enforcement. Again, the realization of one's town or city experiencing a riot will not offer much comfort to behold. *Anyone* – trained professional or otherwise – that actively has to defend persons or property from great harm will find his or her life changed forever.

In our discussion, we shall fuse both protective measures and defensive activities together for convenience, but the reader should understand the intrinsic differences between the two subjects to utilize them properly within his or her personal security program. We may assume that "defense" comes into play when *protection* fails, but this would be somewhat disingenuous. After all, protection against sexually transmitted diseases, for instance, could not possibly defend against attempted rape. In this scenario, the protective element did not break down; it merely offered protection against *another* threat.

At best, your personal protective activities should provide *time* for you to launch into defensive mode. As an example, your local tornado siren may represent your community's protection against the loss of life, but it merely provides you time in order to defend yourself within shelter. From another perspective, your home alarm system may not deter a burglar from breaking into your home, but it should provide you with time to reach for your gun (assuming that your aggressor did not disable the system). When protection cannot provide time for defense specifically, you should have a program in place that allows for a quick and seamless transition between the two elements of security.

For example, your response to an approaching assailant may involve directing your wife and children behind your vehicle (protection) while you simultaneously place your hand upon your concealed firearm (defense). There should be no hesitance between the first action and the second. Passiveness must flow into action without disruption. Herein is where *your* security plan differs from 99% of the planet. Your goal to "survive" must become second nature, *subconscious*, and this requires a great deal of discipline and training.

Consider this for a moment. The brief words that you read within this particular book may have taken a few days or weeks to compose. Yet, this effort – mechanical defects and all – rests upon thirty-four years of professional experience and over fifty years of life experience. And this *only* represents a book. How much experience and life have you placed into your security plan by comparison? Have you formulated a response to any number of the thousands of threats that you are likely to encounter within any given day sufficient to handle the crisis before your conscious mind even understands that there remains a threat to deal with? Again, people do *not* rise to the occasion; they fall upon their *lowest* level of conditioning.

Fortunately, you are your own worst enemy. This means that if you do not affect a proper security plan for your survival preparations, then you have *only yourself* to blame. As far as troubles go, this at least provides you with an opportunity to change your situation around. This would not be the case if you relied exclusively upon taxpayer-funded or external protection. We can ascertain these problems within the following graphic.

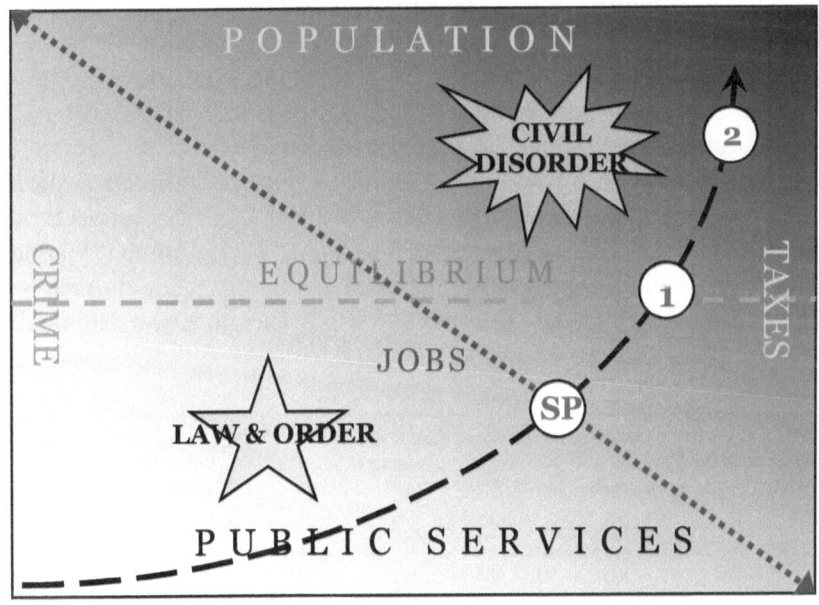

Figure 5. Relationship between population growth, taxes, public services, and crime.

In Figure 5, we observe the relationship between population growth and taxes, and their affect on public services, jobs, and crime. Civil disorder, as we can see, occurs when jobs fall beneath a sustainable level, taxes become too much of a burden on the community, and population growth exceeds an ability to provide adequate public services. To protect against this eventuality, your Security Plan (SP) must be enacted no later than the period where jobs match the provision of municipal services. This point – where individuals lose both his and her sense of entitlement *and* an opportunity to work – is *the most critical point in societal collapse,* even if civil disorder may require more time to incubate.

At this point, you benefit from a period of relative calmness (right before the storm, however) when the public assumes that jobs will soon shift towards the positive, when taxes can still provide law and order, and the population has yet to reach the breaking point. In other words, you are *secure* because most everyone else believes that they are secure. The next evolution exists at Point 1 (Figure 5) when taxes and crime reach equivalent levels while jobs decrease significantly in relation to population growth. Here is where many individuals begin to question what authorities are doing about "the rise in crime" and, certainly, elements of xenophobia appear as much of the city's population growth comes from the addition of newcomers that *may* be blamed for the mounting frustrations of long-term residents.

By this point, you should be making serious efforts to move towards a more peaceful community or, at a very minimum, seeking to store additional supplies and shore up your defensive measures (*protective* measures evaporating by this time). Point 2 represents the crisis period when taxes, population, and crime have reached their saturation limits. Employment remains virtually non-existent and public services significantly behind schedule. Experiencing Point 2 should have you settling into your 'bug out' location for the events that you left behind encroach upon anarchy.

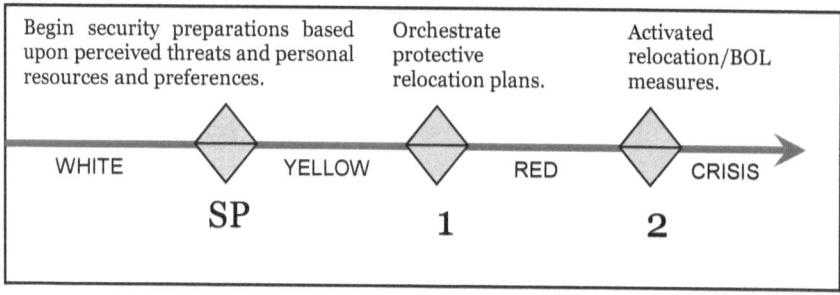

Figure 6. Progression of Security Policies. For crises described in Figure 5.

Figure 6 provides a basic scale for transgression between these points in relation to the intelligence and security awareness issues that we have discussed thus far. Your preparations predate Yellow Intelligence mode and your move to a safer location predates Red Intelligence mode...*ideally*. The truth is, however, that you may have to ride out urban crises wherever you are at that particular moment. Bugging out is *not* an issue for the under-financed or under resourced – conditions that may not always reflect negligence. Let's face it; a secure cabin in the forest may not represent the capability of most individuals.

Our goal within this book remains to offer you ideas on security provisions *wherever* you may find yourself residing and this includes those interminably difficult periods where you find a crisis pitched between you and your security plan. You may have to protect your family, for instance, when you happen to be a great many miles away. Conversely, you may have to defend them when you are located away from your preferred weapons, stores, and vehicles. *Nothing* in life proceeds smoothly and you will often find crises happening during the most inopportune time (which is why they are called *crises* in the first place).

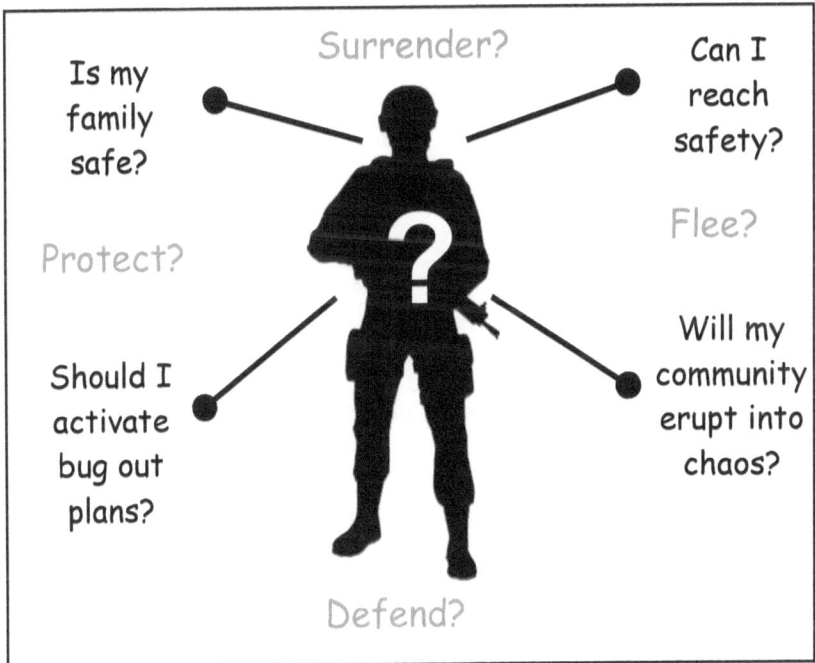

Figure 7. The swirling questions of security.

Your decisions today rest upon thousands of questions that you have undoubtedly asked yourself for years (Figure 7). This merely compounds the problem of implementing protection and defense plans, though the former is likely undertaken during periods of relative peace more so than active defense responses.

In Table 3, we articulate some of the questions that you may have to search for answers to for each element:

Table 3. Protection versus defense.

PROTECTION	DEFENSE
Should my protection option be more mobile? Or stationary?	Will my defense be lethal first, or simply escalate towards lethality?
Will this protection function if neglected for some period?	Will my defense tax resources and personnel too drastically?
How *close* do I need to be to a specific location for this protection to work?	Once deployed, will I be able to cease defensive measures?
How well will the uninitiated understand the function of my protection plan?	Will defense cause too many innocent casualties for the effort?

These do not represent codified questions; rather, they are intended to serve as foundational thoughts for you to build upon when authenticating your own survival strategy.

For example, in considering protective measures, you could very easily determine whether a single activity might fit all four requirements as with auto insurance that 1.) Protects your vehicle both at home and on the road, 2.) Will function unless you fail to make timely payments – which can be eliminated through auto-pay, 3.) Functions whether you are near to your car or not, and 4.) Is readily understandable to all parties. These features are what make insurance so valuable on a number of levels and for a variety of reasons.

When we discuss defensive measures, however, things begin to get a little more complicated. In order to answer all four questions within one activity, the defender is nearly always restricted to the use of firearms.

Here, an individual can elect to shoot to kill or merely hold off an intruder (first question), conserve bullets through training and practice (second question), elect *not* to shoot if, say, an "intruder" turned out to be rather innocuous (third question), and remain tactical enough to avoid collateral damage (fourth question). What makes this option quite complicated involves the very use of firearms – a great many locations throughout the United States and the broader world prevent citizens from possessing firearms.

Any *reduction* within the efficiency of a weapon – say, from a firearm to a knife, or from a knife to bare hands – forfeits a few of the answers. For instance, if you were to pull a knife on an intruder bearing a firearm, you are likely to die and, as a result, not be able to withdraw your posture. Survival requires you to possess a weapon at least one degree more effective than the threat (for example, possession of a thermonuclear missile will likely stave off even battalions of tanks and infantry). Nevertheless, defense within locations hostile to private firearms ownership requires intricate planning and more reliance upon protective measures.

Such provisions may incorporate the following:

- *The employment of group dynamics.* Here, several individuals may be available to confront an armed aggressor from several divergent locations. This would magnify the efficiency of improvised weapons and keep the aggressor off balance.

- *Focus upon intelligence-centric defenses.* With a keen awareness of your community's profile and the activities of individuals within that community, it is possible to become aware of trending threats prior to their arrival at your location.

- *Concentration upon passive activities.* Simply avoiding troublesome areas or periods of the day may reduce chances of confronting aggressive individuals.

- *Acquiescence to public authority.* When all else fails, simply pray that local law enforcement and emergency services are quickly available whenever you need them.

Naturally, these measures remain decidedly inefficient when compared with taking full control of your defensive posture. Unfortunately, however, there are locations where such provisions are warranted due to local legislation or tyrannical leadership.

In such situations, it may behoove you to *violate these laws willingly* – but, naturally, such considerations tip the scales on ethical behavior and should only be used as a last resort (such as when your life hangs in imminent danger). The choice rests entirely with the reader for no one can voluntarily teach another to become a criminal. He or she must weigh the extreme gravity of his or her choice and reflect upon whether that violation of the law was intended to save innocent human lives rather than to harm others – and *then* accept the legal consequences as they may be.

With these prerequisites out of the way, we can now turn to discussion of more active defenses designed to stop aggression against you, your family, and your environment. For practicality – and simplicity – this book focuses upon the preservation of your surroundings whether you represent an individual in transit, a family hunkering down while under attack, or a small group located within a prepared 'bug out' location. As always, you are encouraged to avail yourself of the numerous other books and periodicals on the subject for subsequent learning.

RECOMMENDED READINGS

Bahmanyar, M. (2004). *Afghan Cave Complexes 1979-2004: Mountain Strongholds of the Mujahideen, Taliban, & Al Qaeda.* Oxford (U.K.): Osprey Publishing.

Fowler, M. C. (2005). *Amateur Soldiers, Global Wars: Insurgency and Modern Conflict.* Westport, CT: Praeger Security International.

Godson, R. (2008). *Dirty Tricks or Trump Cards: U.S. Cover Action & Counterintelligence.* New Brunsick (U.S.A.): Transaction Publishers.

Headquarters, Department of the Army. (2002). *FM 3-06 Combined Arms Operations in Urban Terrain.* Washington: Department of the Army.

Poole, H. J. (2003). *The Tiger's Way: A U.S. Private's Best Chance for Survival.* Emerald Isle, NC: Posterity Press.

Poole, H. J. (2007). *Dragon Days: Time for "Unconventional" Tactics.* Emerald Isle, NC: Posterity Press.

Poole, H. J. (2008). *Tequila Junction: 4th-Generation Counterinsurgency.* Emerald Isle, NC: Posterity Press.

Stewart, C. (2012). *Build the Perfect Bug Out Bag: Your 72-Hour Disaster Survival Kit.* Blue Ash, OH: Betterway Home.

U.S. Army Training and Doctrine Command. (2003). *A Military Guide to Terrorism in the Twenty-First Century.* Fort Leavenworth: Deputy Chief of Staff for Intelligence.

United States Department of the Army. (1961). *FM 31-21 Guerrilla Warfare and Special Forces Operations.* Washington: U.S. War Office.

ACTIVE DEFENSE

AT SOME POINT, you will have to defend yourself, your family, or your dwelling physically from aggressive invasion. These assailants may be after your food, your firearms, your stores, or even your women. Whether erupting from a riot, a natural calamity such as a massive hurricane or earthquake, or simply degradation of society, you now represent *law and order* for your little microcosm. This period represents when your security plan becomes doctrine for war and, as such, you remain faced with three immediate questions:

1. ***Are you prepared to defend by any means necessary.*** This is not a rhetorical question. Untold thousands of "preppers" populate the world and virtually every single one of them has not had to kill even an animal to survive. To look at human lives through your own eyes and watch the life drain out of their bodies or, perhaps, even witness those bodies disintegrate rapidly is *not* a normal, modern human action. During most wars where the participants were largely conscripts – which you undoubtedly represent – such as the American Civil War and WWII, a significant percentage of soldiers intentionally fired over the heads of the enemy for fear of killing. During the Battle of Gettysburg, for instance, thousands of muskets were recovered that contained multiple bullets suggesting that soldiers merely wanted to "look" as though they were engaging within combat.

2. ***What are your plans for the "new you"?*** When the bullets start flying – literally or figuratively – *your life* is over, as you understand it. Forget about preparing for the "end of the world as

we know it" – your "world" will disintegrate while the rest of the planet moves on comfortably. Rarely, has any civilization experienced a profound shift towards emerging unrecognizable within the same generation. Even Putin's Russia remains little different from the Soviet Union. The best examples of "profound change" – such as post-Revolution Iran – are extremely rare and even that particular nation may not stay intact for another decade or so. Unfortunately, a decade represents too large a chunk of your life for you to deal with. Therefore, you require a well thought out plan for the transformation that *you* will experience within seconds when the time comes.

3. ***How will you decompress?*** Ancient conflicts, before the era of mechanized standoff weapons, were brutal and bloody battles where individuals literally smelled their enemy. After these battles were over, astute commanders separated the combatants from the main camps and had them clean their swords and shields for several days. One of the main reasons for this ritual was to permit their warriors to wind down before the commander thrust combat experienced personnel into virgin populations. One cannot go from Conan the Barbarian to Mr. Bean overnight. It takes time, deep personal reflection, and a commitment to understand what just transpired before you can permit yourself to deal with family and friends – let alone the public. Following any form of armed defense of your home or environment, you will have to excuse yourself to spend some time away from "home" in order to survive mentally. Failure to do this will simply turn you into a fanatical killer.

We can now discuss these questions in more detail and offer suggestions in what you might do to alleviate problems in the future. As always, the solution rests with your experiences and conscience, plus a healthy dose of research on your part. Few can answer the inconceivable for you; fewer still hold the appropriate experience.

That you are preparing for survival means relatively little if you are not prepared to go all the way. That is, we can surmise, the vast majority of preppers or survivalists bear a psychological limit that keeps him or her from delving into their survival plan one-hundred percent. Even isolationist poster child Ted Kaczynski (a.k.a., the Unabomber) found the need to involve the postal service and global media in with his plans to retaliate against technology. As much as he wanted to avoid the trappings of modern society, his subconscious still found a means to keep the lifeline intact.

For his role, Olympics bomber Eric Rudolph remained on the run for years, but did so more through his local associations than his skill as a survivalist attesting to the inability of people to fully break his or her connection with a community. Nevertheless, these two represented sociopathic criminals that, undoubtedly, incorporated such measures into his plan of action. You, on the other hand, have not been planning to blow up innocent people. In fact, *bombs* are not suitable for *any* survival program.

What you will be confronted with represents a life-and-death battle between you (and your family) and an aggressor. That aggressor will likely have already taken another human life. He or she will also likely suffer from some psychological need that *requires* defeating you at all cost. This may represent an addiction to drugs or simple need for food, but their method of obtaining either is to kill without reflection. That they probably killed in the past to quench this need merely ensures that subsequent murders remain less troubling to them.

Unless you represent a combat veteran or, perhaps, police officer, the chances are negligible that you have harmed another human being in anger. Even your existence as a prepper or survivalist rests upon fear – fear of life more than fear of death. That is, you are afraid to live without food, water, or friendship so you partake of some manner of extending those conveniences. Unfortunately, this is not necessarily a sound rationale for undertaking survival.

To survive, once must be *excited* about life, not merely threatened by the lack of luxuries. One must *value* life more than simply devalue death. You must want to survive for the *potential* of the future rather than regrets emanating from the past. This requires a broad isolation from technologies, entitlements, and preferences. You must gaze upon your life from birth on through perceived end and declare to yourself what it is that you can reasonably *guarantee* and proceed from there. A Corvette in the garage with a young blond wife and 2.5 children is *not* an absolute. Eating just enough food to survive for the day with adequate protection against the elements just may be.

From here, we can determine what it is for which you may be willing to kill. Odds are, it is not for that sports car in the garage. Under all aspects of 'just war' or personal defense, the arguments parallel the precepts of the *Catechism of the Catholic Church*: "Preserving the common good of society requires rendering the aggressor unable to inflict harm." (Paragraph #2266). Neither your sports car nor your home means much to society as a whole. *However*, your life and that of your family's *is*, for without populations, society matters little.

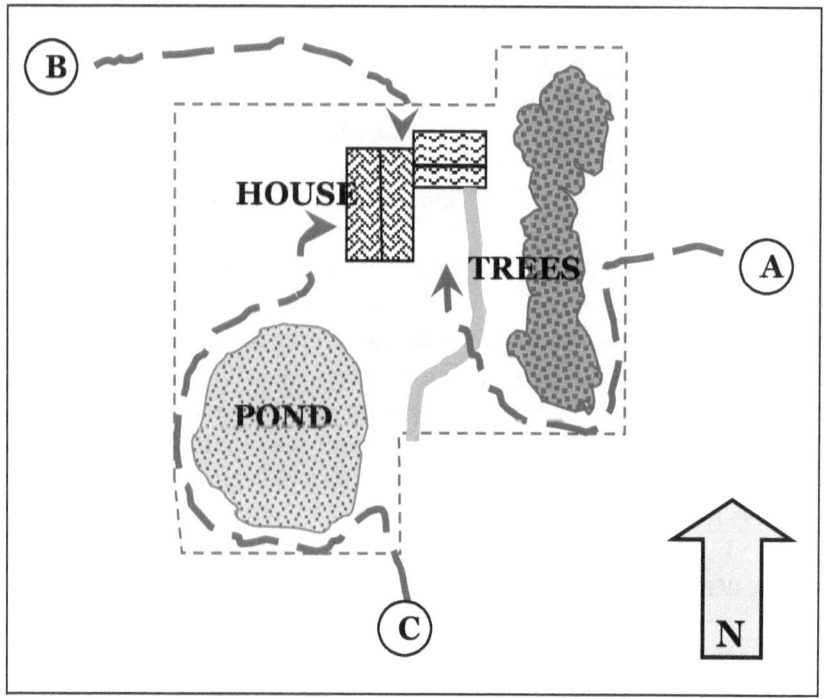

Figure 8. Comparative threats to a home.

Let us review Figure 8 and analyze three potential threats to an average rural home. Individual A is arriving from the west, making a circuit around the trees and heads along the driveway. Individual B is coming in from the north and heads directly towards the rear entrance of the residence. Individual C, instead of walking up the drive, changes course and then circles around the pond to arrive at the side of the house. How would you evaluate these visitors to your home?

While all three bear potential as threats, Individual A is making a seemingly conscious effort to approach the house from the most visible side. If he or she were to be a major threat, it is likely that they would attempt to penetrate your perimeter *through* the woods rather than taking the long way around the trees. Individual B, although approaching from the other side of the residence is likewise making a very visible approach to your home. Perhaps he or she is simply a friendly neighbor who has often arrived at this entry rather than walk completely around to the more formal front entrance. Individual C, however, is *avoiding* all visible approaches to your home, going around the pond away from the driveway and then approaching your house from the side with the least chances of finding a door. In fact, their path abruptly shifted away from the driveway – perhaps he or she saw movement within the house and elected to divert away from the front?

In reality, *all three individuals* could be threatening to your safety and security. That said, perception of threat escalates with each individual's mannerism – rising from low (A) to moderate (B) to high (C). Despite this, Individual B holds the *least* warning because he or she is approaching from the short end of your home. That is, your property line towards the north is very near to the home and faces to the rear of the house, making any causal glances towards this area less than towards the front. For all his or her suspicious activity, Individual C is within plain view – unless the pond holds high embankments.

In any of these cases, one cannot simply begin shooting – or even request the individual to cease and desist without probable cause. Among the myriad of potentialities remain federal agents serving arrest warrants to the wrong house (as has happened before) but in that case, individuals would have to be moving in from several locations simultaneously and not merely one trespasser. It is further hoped that such a systematic approach by multiple individuals would lead you to only one of two scenarios: the aforementioned assault by the "good guys" or a coordinated attack upon your home by criminals seeking profitable ventures.

Herein, again, you must be prepared to fight or surrender with minimal time for options. Presumably, you have lived your life honorably, so this reduces (but not eliminates) the possibilities for errant police presence. Therefore, the approach of several individuals means that your comfortable dwelling or 'bug out' location is under aggression. Now what, you ask? This is where security definitely shifts from protection to defense and measures from passive to active. If society is collapsing due to a major crisis, then you must fall back upon your primal "defend at all cost" plan of action. Yet, herein, we find ourselves again dealing with a complicated list of considerations to review.

Let us suppose, for a moment, that a riot has broken out in your community and you find dozens of thugs running helter-skelter down your driveway towards your front door. Your first reaction might be one of grabbing your gun and shooting the individuals prior to their reaching your house. Conversely, perhaps you simply grab your wife and kids and head towards your safe room. A third option might be to hold your firearm within your hands and *hope* that the crowd thinks twice about entering your premises. What we have failed to consider, however, rests with the events leading to your home's invasion.

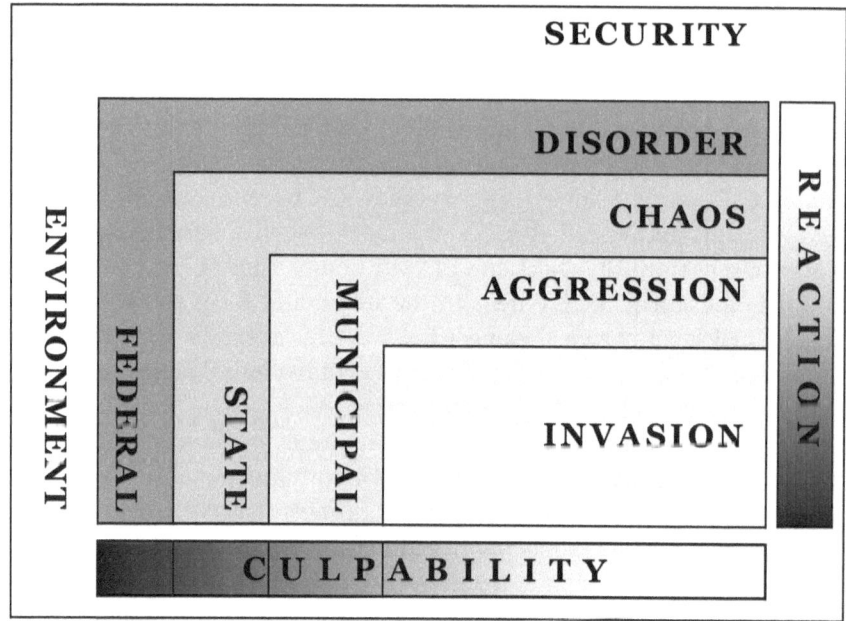

Figure 9. Relationship between response and culpability.

The events surrounding your environment may appear as if the world is coming unglued and this assessment would be correct if not for one important consideration – the rest of your community, state, or nation may be purring along as if nothing out of the ordinary is transpiring. What this means is that if you begin firing away at the dozen or so individuals attacking your home, you will likely face significant legal (and criminal) issues with everyone from your local mayor on up through the national judicial agency of your nation. On the other hand, if your country was situated within a full blown civil war, then there remains little doubt that you will proceed through such a crisis relatively unhindered (unless *your side* loses).

Figure 9 illustrates this reality in graphical terms. Actions taken during broader conditions tend to increase your culpability. For instance, if your country is merely experiencing political disorder – as, say, during a disputed election cycle – any armed defense upon your part will draw the full weight of that national authority upon you. Because of the situation, your need to defend (react) remains relatively low. On the other hand, if your home is being invaded directly, your reaction time is very critical and, therefore, you may see less culpability – yet this will not absolve you completely. You will have to prove that the progression of federal, state, and municipal services were not suitable for your particular environment. Furthermore, you will have to present a substantial case that your action was commensurate with the threat.

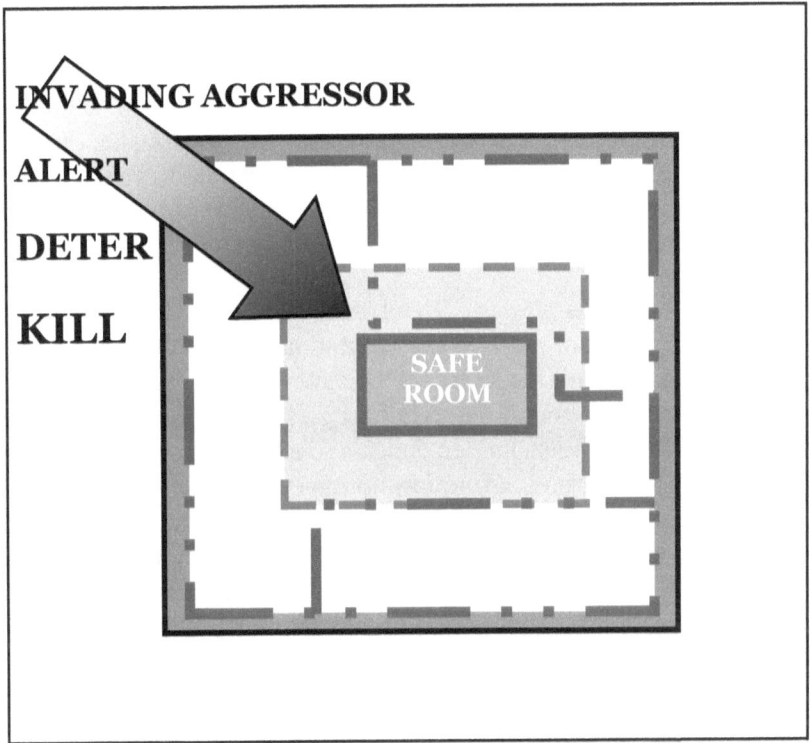

Figure 10. Progression of response.

In Figure 10, we observe the progression in detail. An aggressor first enters a property, forcing the resident to retreat to his or her safe room. In this regard, the resident must simply call for police and alert them to the situation, preferably through some manner of panic button. When the aggressor proceeds further into the property, passive measures are enforced, such as the location of the resident's safe room. These measures are largely structural and are designed into the property. If the aggressor keeps moving towards the safe room and actually locates the compartment, then any further escalation of the invasion requires the killing of the intruder lest the resident and/or his or her family rest in imminent danger.

This portion of our discussion is relatively straightforward and should be considered common sense. However, we must still dissect this scenario to discuss the appropriate measures for each escalating threat.

Alert status. Whenever any suspicious individual or individuals appear upon your property, the first reaction that you must do (insofar as practical) is to alert the authorities. Preferably, you will possess a security alarm panic button (*protection*) that will enable you to retreat towards your safe room (*defense*). This option avoids the troubling time that it takes to dial the local emergency number and explain your situation. If an alarm system is not available, then you should have both cordless landline and cellular telephone services to call for aid once you retreat to your protective room. Here, you will further have possession of your chosen firearm for escalated threat deterrence.

Deter status. In this scenario, deterrence represents largely a passive defense. Your safe room must be easy to find and access for you and your family, but quite difficult for intruders to locate. This capitalizes on the one thing that *all* intruders share – unfamiliarity with your surroundings. You can fashion false stairwells, hidden doors, and a range of other options that delay aggressors from finding your location. As police response times range from 15-45 minutes, depending upon your precise community, then this serves as the period that you must delay intruders during the deter phase: 45 minutes. Beyond that and you are safe; less than this time and you may have to resort to the next level.

Kill status. If the intruder discovers your safety location, perhaps if a group of individuals are attacking your home and they see your family flee into the safe room, then you have effectively retreated far enough for most municipalities to conclude that *you* were not acting within the aggressor role. Here is where you possess little options but to take down the aggressor(s) with lethal force. Even within such a basic schematic as in Figure 10, just about anyone would conclude that these belligerents worked their way *too* far into your premises for merely burglary. When people chase you *that* far into your home – right up to your safe room – they have undoubtedly transcended your calls to the police and all deterrence measures. In this situation, *someone* is voluntarily forfeiting his or her lives – do not let it be you.

We have now reached the subject matter of this particular chapter – and our discussion has only just begun.

The military concept of "personal force protection" means to protect you, your family, and your home from all manners of threat, to include terrorism. We have simply acknowledged that concept to include all means necessary to achieve this objective. Now, we must discuss *how* to employ lethal force properly as the case may be, for this very topic will tug at societal concepts of ethics, religion, politics, and sociology amongst others.

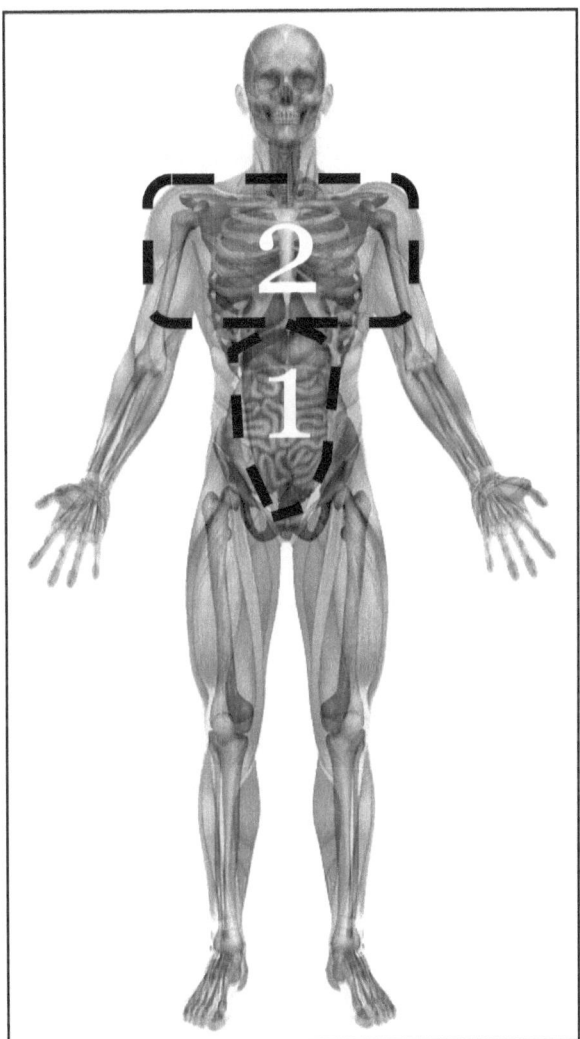

Figure 11. Human vulnerabilities. © AlienCat - Fotolia.com Consolidated image: R.J. Godlewski

Of the numerous human vulnerabilities (and decided lack thereof), only two target areas should be considered by anyone defending his or her home and family. These are identified within Figure 11 and are provided in order of preference. That is, Target #1 contains an individual's midsection and includes the stomach, intestines, and other soft organs that, when injured, provide substantial damage to the human person. This target area is also among the easiest to hit when shooting under duress. Target #2 covers an individual's lungs and heart, but the rib cage protects these organs. Furthermore, only the heart serves as a singular organ and extensive damage to one lung will not incapacitate the aggressor.

Figure 12. Masterpiece Arms MPA-10T in .45 ACP. © 2015, R.J. Godlewski.

To render an aggressor unable to inflict any degree of harm, successfully, requires two objectives. First, the aggressor needs to be hit with as much bullet mass as possible. Second, this bullet mass has to hit enough vital organs to stop the attacker before they reach your person or a loved one. In this statement, we are furthering dispensing with two counter arguments from both professionals and critics. One, we can dismiss outright the thought of "only needing one or two bullets" to defeat an aggressive individual. Human beings have been known to withstand as many as five or six hits and *still* been able to kill a victim. Two, experts argue for immediate incapacitation through targeting the aggressor's second and third vertebrae, but such precision is difficult for even the best-trained marksman working with a *stationary target*. Your aggressor is likely to be *moving*.

Now we must consider the environment under which you are likely to be shooting at an aggressor. In essence, you will be confronted with an urban warfare environment where the battle will take place within your living room, kitchen, bedroom, etc. – rooms within your residence that warrant extreme care as opposed to shootings undertaken on the open plains. This will require you to employ ammunition specifically designed for inside shooting, including the .45 ACP pistol caliber and the 5.56mm rifle caliber.

Figure 13. DPMS/Panther Arms AP4 in 5.56x45mm. © 2015 R.J. Godlewski.

In Figures 12 and 13, we observe two firearms representative of these calibers and for which frangible ammunition remains widely available, meaning that the bullets will shatter upon contact with any dense object. These bullets will still penetrate drywall and similar construction materials, but they will not ricochet off metal, tile, or other dense items found within your home. The advantage of the MPA pistol is that it fires the massive .45 ACP round that remains a proven 'man stopper' bullet. It is also easier to maneuver with or without its optional barrel extension (see Figure 14). Both firearms carry 30-round magazines providing exceptional firepower for force protection.

Another firearm that deserves merit – primarily for its ease of use and availability – represents the Kalashnikov AKM (Modernized AK-47) family, especially its folding stock AKMS version (see Figure 15), which is considered a pistol within the United States. This firearm, chambered within the venerable 7.62 x 39mm cartridge, can take a literal beating and keep on functioning. It remains simple enough that virtually *any* shooter can learn to operate it within a matter of hours (for those family members that may have to come to *your* aid).

Figure 14. MPA-10T without optional barrel extension. © 2015 R.J. Godlewski

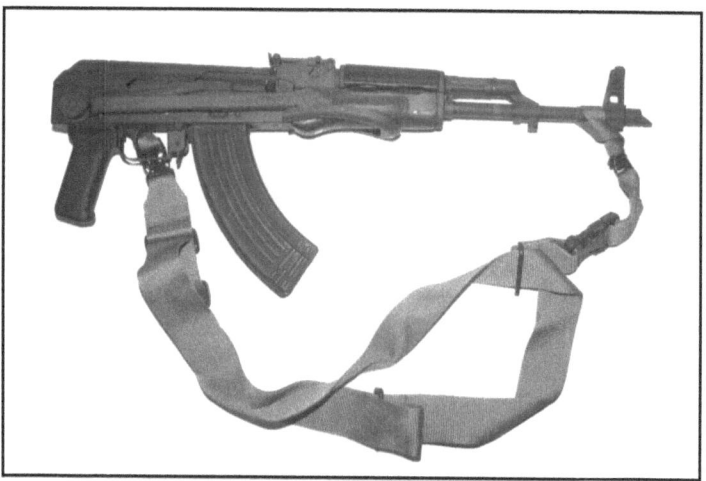

Figure 15. AKMS in 7.62 x 39mm. © 2015, R.J. Godlewski

In a less urban setting, the Kalashnikov may very well represent the best option for its larger caliber bullet remains superior to the AR-15's 5.56 mm round, which experiences trouble going through dense vegetation and glass. It also comes within a wide variety of styles (see Figure 16) and more modernized versions contain several of the options normally associated with AR-15 rifles (see Figure 17).

Figure 16. Hungarian AMD-65 (AK-47) in 7.62 x 39mm. ©
2015, R.J. Godlewski

**Figure 17. Ruger SR-556 in 6.8 SPC caliber with optional
accessories.** © 2015, R.J. Godlewski

Any of the firearms depicted herein offer the advantages of size,
firepower, and flexibility necessary to protect one's home and his or her
family from harm. Unfortunately, those residing in areas where "assault
weapons" are illegal, a shift in firepower is required. Fortunately, those
unfortunate individuals can still pack a powerful punch, one diverse in its
application.

A .12 gauge shotgun arguably remains the most popular home
defense gun on the planet and the number of options available is
staggering. One of the more unique variants, in recent years, represents the

Mossberg JIC (Just in Case) line of "survival" shotguns. In Figure 18, we can see the company's JIC II offering that comes in a takedown version enclosed within a nylon case. This case can be mounted to virtually any backpack or stored within the home.

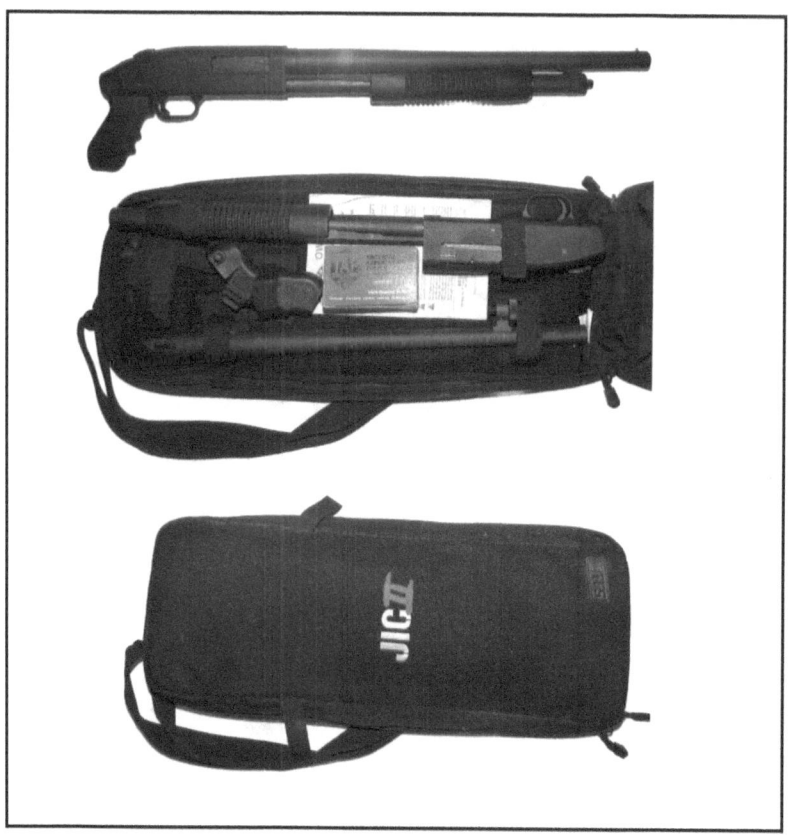

Figure 18. Mossberg JIC II takedown shotgun. Assembled (top), stored (middle), closed case (bottom). © 2015, R.J. Godlewski.

With a range of shell options, the user of a shotgun can fire OO Buckshot, rubber bullets, door breacher rounds, tear gas, and any number of specialized shells designed for a multitude of lethal and non-lethal mission requirements. Conceivable, a shooter can chamber a mixture of flash bang, rubber batons, and buckshot within the same firearm to handle rapidly escalating situations. However, it is recommended that you keep your firearm loaded with tactical quality buckshot and employ the ageless axiom that if you have to point your weapon at someone, then they are going to die.

Figure 19. Taurus 24/7 OSS in .45 ACP. Recently replaced with second-generation 24/7s. © 2015, R.J. Godlewski

When traveling between your home and various destinations, nothing can match the raw power and concealability of a .45 ACP pistol (see Figure 19). Possessing anywhere from eight to thirteen rounds, a good quality, tactical pistol may mean the difference between life and death when you are caught in crises far from home or your 'bug out' location. Whatever firearm you possess, however, your training and education within its use requires daily application – *not* yearly or monthly, but every day must be spent on proficiency training.

Your job as protector of your family rests with your ability to sneak through life as a warrior – *not* erupt as a terrorist or maniacal criminal. If you cannot pass yourself off as a gentle person to your neighbors and friends, then they will suspect duplicity on your part. This could lead to as many problems as if you were to broadcast the fact that you are a prepper, survivalist, or however you prefer to call someone that tries to live just a little bit longer than the sheep that inhabit the earth.

Security provides you with the mechanism for certainty, but *only* if you are conscious of the "grave duty" that self-defense entails. You own firearms, for example, not because you expect to use them, but because you are *prepared* to employ them if necessary. The same holds true with your transition from *protection* to *defense*. God forbid should you ever have to believe that you might have to use a rifle, shotgun, or pistol to defend yourself or your family. Such actions represent the *breakdown* of security, not its primary purpose. That said, you bear the confidence that if *anyone* pulls a weapon on you – *you* will emerge as the victor. Not the aggressor.

Active defense means that you train enough to understand how to use the *tools* of the trade and firearms are just another instrument within the toolbox. You owe it to society to remain proficient in security, proficient in defense, and, lastly, proficient in exercising extreme prejudice. You may not enjoy training with firearms on a daily basis, but the alternative can be even more unnerving:

Figure 20. When firearms are not available...

RECOMMEND READINGS

Balor, P. (1988). *Manual of the Mercenary Soldier*. Boulder: Paladin Press.

Gander, T. (1990). *Guerrilla Warfare Weapons: The Modern Underground Fighter's Armoury*. New York: Sterling Publishing Co., Inc.

Grossman, D. A. (1993). Defeating the Enemy's Will: The Psychological Foundations of Maneuver Warfare. In J. e. Richard D. Hooker, *Maneuver Warfare: An Anthology*. Novato, CA: Presidio Press.

Kahaner, L. (2007). *AK-47: The weapon that changed the face of war*. Hoboken: John Wiley & Sons, Inc.

Machine, G. (2011). *Israeli Security Warrior Training*. Boulder: Paladin Press.

Paladin Press. (1993). *KGB Alpha Team Training Manual: How the Soviets Trained for Personal Combat, Assassination, and Subversion*. Boulder: Paladin Press.

YOUR (GULP!) BRAVE NEW WORLD

THE ONE THING certain about the world is that it will always be populated by those who declare, "The world is coming to an end!"And, consistently, they have *never* been correct. Those great societies that experienced earth-shattering convulsions – Greece, Rome, Egypt, the Soviet Union, etc. – never realized what it was that they were experiencing until long after the crisis ended. Neither the American Revolution nor even its subsequent Civil War caught citizens off guard.

Yes, these cultures no longer exist, and a great many today will disappear in the future, but human life will continue to go on. Even during today's political "revolutions", taxicabs still operate, airports remain open, and trains continue to chug along. Perhaps if the world simply stepped back and drew in a deep breath, there would be less "end of the world as we know it" people running around screaming that both hell and high water were at your door.

The truth is, however, that we have more to fear from the fear-mongers than we do from our avowed enemies. This is because when the boy cried "Wolf!" in the fable one too many times, he ended up eaten alive. The Islamic jihadists and narco-traffickers that poison our planet, actually *do* want to see us cry wolf one too many times, for such hysteria simply aids their cause. They want us to transform our lives *from* preparedness into complacency rather than the other way around. In fact, so many people are getting rich from the "prepper" craze; you have to wonder just *who* the field's greatest investors are.

You are reading this book because, frankly, you seek *security* more than surviving the latest "earth shattering disaster" conjured up by the likes of Hollywood, and security, as we have already discussed, represents *certainty*. For this reason, this book dispenses with much of the material contained within a thousand other books – some good, some... – that fill survivor's libraries the world over. Despite popular opinion, the world "as we know it" may go on for a great many decades before anything close to testing survival comes into play.

If you are in at least your fifties, for instance, you grew up thinking that the Soviet Union and the United States were on the verge of annihilating us off the planet through nuclear war. Today, the Soviet Union does not even exist, but a resurgent Russia is doing its best to restore the Tsarist order (with new royalty dominated by Moscow-based organized crime). If you grew up during the late 1960s and early 1970s, you witnessed more than your share of terrorists, airliner bombings, and hostage situations. Except then leftist groups did all the troublemaking. Today, leftists seem content on ignoring terrorism as if, somehow, they hold copyright to the tactic.

What is different between our world and today's facsimile is that modern data communications have all but evaporated the lines between "us" and "them". No longer can portions of the world remain isolated from one another to usher in a false sense of *security*. What happens during the 21st century does not remain ineffective – for the slightest disturbances can quickly cause *you* anxiety and – *voila!* – there goes your concept of security. Take a good look at your survival stores and you will understand – does any *sane* individual store food away for decades? Well, yes – and no.

Sane people store bandages for injuries, keep flashlight batteries fresh for when the power eventually goes out, and do not tell anyone what his or her bank account numbers are. These are very *basic* survivalist functions, though we often think of them as merely "common sense". Accordingly, is it senseless, therefore, to retain food for when supplies run low or plan for mountain refuges when tempers run high? Much depends upon how you view preparation.

If you count yourself amongst the rational-minded people of the planet, then your preparations are little more than contingency planning – a little extra here or a slightly more there *just in case*. Preparation for you is not *paranoia* anymore than you keep the SUV locked in the garage as soon as you purchase auto insurance for it. Some people go through his or her entire lives without *ever* filing a claim. Others apparently pay for huge office buildings through his or her premiums and a great many insurance representatives just love betting on how high they can fling that individual's policy costs.

Perhaps, too, we can make the argument that no sane individual would truly want to live during a period of the world ending as we know it, for people remain social creatures that prefer the status quo – otherwise, we would have ditched our politicians centuries ago. What keeps us grounded within the "prepper" craze has more to do with more people than fewer resources. Let us face it, people naturally hate one another. If Dr. Stanley Milgram was correct, more than six out of every ten individuals wants to kill us given an opportunity. At least electrocute us into submission – which is basically the result of the Yale University studies. And a great many people would rather be shot than electrocuted.

Save for the basic human element discussed within Chapter 2, this book avoided the expected concentration on *survival*, which, in and of itself, does not warrant any great admiration. Bacteria survive. Taxes survive. People on welfare survive. Humans were meant to *succeed*. Just read Matthew Chapter 25 about wasting one's life away on the status quo. It is quite fitting that the only apostle to have worked as a tax collector would record Christ's words about mere survival. Our discussion within this book, to the contrary, remains about *security* – not whether you will be able to thaw out *pierogis* in twenty or thirty years – and this means that you want to *save* life as you know it for as long as you can savor it.

Thus far, you have discovered that:

- Security represents a frame of mind, not a physical or procedural doctrine.

- Societies periodically break down, often through the actions of comparatively few individuals.

- Survival, colloquially speaking, is humanity's *first* course of action.

- Intelligence places you at great advantage over others whereas counterintelligence places your adversaries at great disadvantage.

- Protection is a largely passive discipline that functions in your absence.

- Defense is almost exclusively an active discipline that functions in your presence.

- Most preppers will eventually dismiss preparation.

- There is no such thing as the world ending as we know it (for we know so little about the world).

Admittedly, these are not profound revelations, but they remain instrumental in formulating your security strategy.

Your security plan itself rests upon three distinct platforms:

1. ***Security rests with your activities alone.*** You cannot rely upon outsiders to affect security. The police, at best, remain 15 to 45 minutes away. If it takes 3-5 minutes for an aggressor to invade your premises, then that provides them with 10 to 40 minutes to do as they please *before* aid arrives.

2. ***Security means more than mere protection.*** Protection represents perception. Defense requires substance. A firearm, for instance, offers no value until placed into use. At some point, even awareness of its presence will not deter a criminal or intruder. In and of itself, it remains little more than a screwdriver without a screw to drive.

3. ***Security is not about keeping your life from being changed, it is about protecting certainty.*** The number of things that could irreversibly alter your life "as you know it" is almost infinite. Any one of these incidents *will* change your life from that moment onwards. Security, therefore, is not intended to protect your life from change. Rather, it exists to provide you with a fair degree of certainty of what will happen to you *after* such incidents occur.

To implement these requires a lifelong devotion and commitment to the concept of self-preservation (which is not, incidentally, the same thing as survival).

In a world where Bigfoot and zombies are considered real creatures and any unexplained light in the sky becomes an intergalactic visitor, it should not surprise anyone that a great many survivalists and preppers have defeated the purpose of security and force protection. At best, these individuals have morphed into recluses ignorant of the multitude of human beings that will survive even the grandest disruption of "life as we know it". At worst, he or she simply devolves into part of a criminal militia – organized or simply controlled through similar beliefs – that purports preparation to launch a new "citizens government" once the world falls apart.

You, however, understand that both approaches remain detrimental to your position as a functioning member of society. *Your* goal in life is not to fundamentally transform yourself into some form of modern Beowulf, but to keep the rest of your community from descending into hell. After all, seeds *will* be planted to launch a new world following any major catastrophe and you cannot trust that others will be equally supportive of traditional values.

Now, let us revisit that new, secured life of yours in the context of preparations for survival. Your "new" you – or, at a minimum, your revitalized persona – invokes the following:

- ✓ *Every* action that you take, no matter how seemingly irrelevant, displays a *specific purpose*. There remain no wasted motions, no superficial thoughts, no unproductive associations. You possess no "leisure" time; rather, you use free time to further your knowledge, your objectives, and your interests.

- ✓ Survival is *not* about longevity. It is about keeping the status quo intact. You, however, want to *succeed*. This means that while others plan to keep the status quo intact after a major crisis, *you* want to emerge from that catastrophe in better shape than everyone else. Your post-event condition will be as comparably superior as your pre-event intentions.

- ✓ Your security plan does not simply entail bunkering down within a mountain refuge loaded for bear. On the contrary, your security plan represents a sphere that radiates out from you wherever you go. Others may sit and wait for apocalyptic battles, but you simply move through chaos with the confidence that *only* practical security can provide.

- ✓ You function under the highest standards of ethics. You are *not* a fanatic, a "loser", a loner, or a renegade. You are, essentially, a compassionate, caring, family person that simply wants to acknowledge that there is *more* to life than simply reaching a certain age.

These are not necessarily "survivalist" or "prepper" ideals, but you are not your typical survivalist or prepper either. You want *security* within life – not a battle with the world's worst individuals. Yours is a determination to *succeed* – not a war to outlast others. You do not want to plan for the "end of the world as we know it". Rather, you want to be the seed that keeps that world, as we currently understand it, alive for others to benefit from.

Because of this, your concepts of life and security – as with survival and defense – remain more intuitive than most. Your house is not a castle with ramparts, but a sanctuary with integrity. You move about, not restricted through fear, but confident with certainty. You do not simply expect to live a long and prosperous life, you *want* to live a long and prosperous life befitting one whose education (autodidactic and formal), income (work and entrepreneurial), and family life rests absolute. This, folks, represents the truest function of security.

ABOUT THE AUTHOR

R.J. Godlewski (Pronounced *GOD LESS KEY*) is the chief executive manager for a threat resolution services company and serves as president of an international security corporation practicing Fourth-Generation Corporate Security (4GCS) doctrine. He holds an M.A. in Military Studies, Asymmetrical Warfare and a B.A. in Intelligence Studies, Terrorism Studies, both of which earned with honors from American Military University. Mr. Godlewski also holds formal academic training in explosive ordnance disposal and security management and is an honorably discharged veteran of the U.S. Navy and U.S. Navy Reserve.

His previous books include:

Communities at War: Defending Our Schools, Hospitals, and Houses of Worship in the 21st Century

Practical Guerrilla Warfare

Fourth-Generation Corporate Security: Asymmetrical Warfare for Protective Services Professionals

Mini-Manual of the Independent Counterterrorist, Third Edition

Skills of the Assassin: Understanding the Tactics of the Professional Killer

Targeting Narco-Submarine Networks through Deep Penetration, Autonomous Maritime Irregular Warfare Units Operating within a Hunter-Killer Role

www.ingramcontent.com/pod-product-compliance
Lightning Source LLC
Chambersburg PA
CBHW030525290526
45786CB00004B/1629